I am my child's ADVOCATE

by JulieAnn Holland, Ph.D.

Dedication

To my mother, Betty Leasure, my greatest advocate. Thank you mom for advocating for me every day of my life. Thank you for being tough when I needed it and compassionate when I didn't feel I could carry the load on my own any more. Thank you for teaching me how to be a good mother and wife. I know that I can do anything and survive anything because of you. I love you mom!

I Am My Child's Advocate © Copyright 2010 by JulieAnn Holland, Ph.D. All rights reserved. No part of this book may be used or reproduced in any many without written permission. For information, contact JulieAnn Holland at: mychildshealth@gmail.com.

ISBN 978-0-9846088-9-8

To the Reader

The information in this book does not diagnose nor prescribe. This information is not a substitute for personal care and services of a qualified physician. This information is provided for those who are willing to share responsibility for their own health, in conjunction with their physicians. It is important that before beginning any new program, you should always consult with your doctor to be sure that the program fits with your medical regimen.

This book should not be misconstrued to mean or imply that the programs or information described cure any symptom. Becoming educated in living a healthy lifestyle can help you discover the path to optimal health. These statements have not been evaluated by the FDA.

Every effort has been made to ensure that the information contained in this book is accurate and complete. However, some of the information contained is strictly the opinion of the author and based on her life experiences. Neither the author nor the publisher is responsible for any loss or damage allegedly arising from any information or suggestion in this book.

Every effort has been made to provide accurate Internet addresses and references at the time of publication, however, neither the author nor the publisher assume any responsibility for errors or for changes that occur after publication.

Acknowledgements

I would like to thank **my husband, Allen**, who never thought I was "weird" when I told him I was going to go on a live food diet to get well. He detoxed with me and always supported my efforts to help our children be healthier. I love you madly!

I want to thank **my children**, who along with my husband, did the Candida program with a smile so that Bronson could get well. Thank you to my children **Madison, Hannah, and Bronson**, who dutifully take their support supplements and have learned to read labels and care about their bodies. A special thank you to Bronson, for sharing your story and journey so that other families can have hope that health can return and wellness is possible.

Thank you to my dear friend and colleague, **Dr. Linda Nelson**, who mentored me and inspired me to help myself to be well. I thank you for the opportunity to learn and to help so many others gain the knowledge necessary to change their lives. It has been a magnificent journey!

Thank you to **my sisters**, all five of them, who are fierce advocates for their children. They are good mothers and great examples of how to weather the storms of parenting and still smile.

Thank you **Carolyn**, my Ya Ya, for sharing the motherhood journey with me, while we whine, laugh, cry and triumph together!

Inspirational Acknowledgements

Dr. Wayne Dyer: Thank you for sharing your daughter's story about her bumps. If my sister hadn't heard this story, then I would have had an even greater struggle with my son's health. Thank you so very much!

Dr. Laura Schlessinger: Thank you for advocating for moms to be at home with their children. Thank you for stating, "I am my kid's mom or dad." I was inspired to implement this in my quest for advocating for my children in every situation possible each day. Thank you for reaching out among the thorns to fertilize the beautiful roses.

Jenny McCarthy: Thank you for sharing your voice of experience and hope to all those parents who are hanging on by a thread. Hope is everything! Hope is power and inspiration to change and move from our comfort zone and you have reached out and pulled up many from despair. The blessing of Evan's story is hope itself.

Oprah Winfrey: Thank you for your fierce advocacy for children all over the world. You stand as a beacon of golden light over so much darkness and hardship. I deeply admire how you not only speak about advocacy, you lead with shining example. I am grateful for you and pray that your example will keep inspiring others to advocate for children everywhere.

Eunice Kennedy Shriver: Thank you for paving the way for so many children who had opportunities to thrive because you cared and advocated for them. You were a grand lady and a pioneer for the disadvantaged and disabled. Your steadfast work has improved the lives of countless children.

Maria Shriver: Thank you for carrying forth the good example of your mother. You uplift women and empower them to be better mothers so that we can advocate for our children. You said: "When all is said and done, my main goal in life is to raise children who feel they are deeply loved…children who are kind, compassionate and aware of the world around them. If I can do that, I will consider myself a success." That is part of advocacy. Thank you!

Daren and Barbara Jensen: Thank you for being so rock solid in your beliefs regarding Parker and standing your ground to help your child. You went to the ends of the earth to advocate for your child in the face of injustice and persecution. You are truly advocates for your children and have inspired others to be stronger. Your story helped me to think, reconsider, and evaluate advocating for children, and in the end become more steadfast.

Mother Teresa: Thank you for advocating for all of us!

Unknown Faces and Unheard Voices: I know you are out there advocating, so thank you! Let's ban together and help each other's children. The power of advocacy is endless when we reach out and share our knowledge and provide hope.

Table of Contents

1. **Bronson's Story** 10
2. **What Is Candida?** 16
   - Self-Test for Candida 16
   - The Holistic Approach to Treating Candida 19
   - What You CAN Eat on the Candida Program 23
   - Foods NOT Permitted During the Candida Program 23
   - Sample Candida Meal Plan 24
   - M'lis Candida Program Calendar 29
3. **Earning Your Health; Good, Bad, And Really Bad** 31
   - Degenerative Diseases Not Known of or Diagnosed Before 1950 32
   - M'lis Immune System Recovery Calendar 34
   - Common Immune System Disorders Improved by the Immune System Recovery Plan 35
   - Summary of Juicing Basics 35
   - In-Depth Juicing 35
   - The Use of Juices Within the Body ....
4. **Womb For Improvement** 40
   - Especially for Men 41
   - Pre-Prenatal and Prenatal Health: For Men and Women ....
   - Hormones in Women 44
   - Questions to Ask Yourself During Pregnancy 45
   - Induced Labor 47
5. **Rights And Insights** 51
   - Good Fertilizer 52
   - Bad Weeds 53
6. **The Myth Of Instant Gratification** 55
   - The Sufferer 56
   - The Arguer 57
   - The Doer 57
   - The "Aha Moment" 58
   - Pure Belief is Powerful 58

7. The Medication Craze 60
Ritalin: The Big Lie 60
Psychiatric Medications Taken by Children 62
Food Pyramid 64
Cost, Inconvenience, and Rewards 66

8. Environmental Healing And Challenges 67
The School Rule 69
The Ex-Challenge 72

9. Powerful Parenting 74
The Power Of Always 74
The Power of Prayer 75
The Unique Circumstances of Trials 76
Advocating by Using our Talents 76

10. Parenting With A Purpose 78
Gratitude for Grandparents 78
Roadblocks 79
Normal Stuff is Good Stuff 80
Keeping Yourself Healthy 81
Summary 82

References 84

Forword

I often entertain myself in the car by listening to Dr. Laura's radio program. Again and again, I hear callers stating, "I am my kid's mom or dad." I have always thought that this was such a cheesy saying, but I admit it is very catchy, as hundreds of women and men are now using this phrase. How many of these parents are really backing these words with deeds? I don't know, however, I suspect most of them are truly trying their best to navigate the winding and treacherous roads of parenthood.

I was inspired to put these words into action due to some unique experiences I have had over the years with my own children, as well as children of my friends and clients. The past few years I keep hearing myself tell others, "I am my child's advocate." It sounds a lot like the Dr. Laura phrase, doesn't it? Am I cheesy too? Maybe a little, but these words are packed with power and love that knows no bounds and that is impossible to describe to anyone, including myself.

My experiences may be of little importance to some, possibly of mild interest to others, and some may even see a mirror image of themselves and their experiences as they read my words. I am going to share mine with the hope that you might connect with some of the information I present. Making the right connections in life with people, information, and most importantly with God, helps us live life in the most successful and joyful way possible.

Almost twenty years ago, I began my career as a paramedical esthetician. In this role, I provided esthetic procedures to burn victims, cancer patients, and other individuals with disorders of the skin. As a Master Esthetician, I began providing micro pigmentation procedures, specializing in areolas for breast cancer survivors. By the way, these people are some of my favorite clients, because of their zest for life and sheer will to overcome great trials. I finally completed a Bachelors Degree program three weeks before I gave birth for the first time, emerging with a Bachelors of Science in Business Administration and Management. I was later inspired to go back to school to complete a Naturopathic Doctorate and a Ph.D. in natural health. I love to learn and I enjoy having opportunities to share some of the most important ideas I have learned with others through lectures, classes, individual consultations, and now this book.

After my last child was born, I came up against some personal and unique health challenges. I was diagnosed with Fibromyalgia, a debilitating auto-immune disorder, and Candida, an over-infestation of yeast in the body. I had already been suffering with Endometriosis for over fifteen years. My husband thought that I was losing my mind because nobody could be sick all the time. I had doctor's even go so far as to suggest that I have bones removed from my spine to relieve migraine headaches. Fortunately, I wasn't desperate enough to try this tactic. I did, however, have a CAT Scan for a potential brain tumor, which turned out to be nothing, but it sure cost something!

None of the testing provided any answers. At this point, something remarkable happened that would change my life forever. My parents bought a house a couple of miles up the road from mine. Some may think that this sounds like a nightmare rather than a miracle. Depending on your personal outlook on life, I suppose it could be either. I am constantly reminding myself and others: "Your attitude, your choice", which I will elaborate on later in the book. In my case, it was a miracle. Not only did I have a terrific support system, but my parents unknowingly chose neighbors who would affect my life and my posterity for generations.

We were visiting with my parents at their new home one evening when there was a knock at the door. My parent's invited in their new neighbors, Bill and Dr. Linda Nelson. Dr. Nelson is a Naturopath, a person who studies and implements the natural healing of the mind, body, and spirit. She took one look at me and knew how sick I was, and then proceeded to tell me that I could be symptom free in six months, if I wanted to be well. Of course I wanted to be well! I later learned that not everyone chooses to be well if given the option (as discussed later in the book), but I was absolutely ready to change the way that I felt! I was well versed in nutrition, and the information I was given by Dr. Nelson, fit right in with what I had been unsuccessfully trying to do on my own. She was right, and I was well in about six months. Her council and support changed my life, forever altering my course and enhancing my life's journey.

Little did I know, this new way of life, would become a life long journey. Sometimes I think I have created my own little Pandora's Box. This is when I decided to go back to school to pursue a doctorate in natural health care and go on to receive an N.D, Ph.D. I have owned and operated several natural health spas and clinics over the years, building a very successful private practice. I now educate and lecture for over seventy-five different health spas, clinics and wellness centers all over the country. I do this alongside my good friend Dr. Linda Nelson, because I hired myself at her company and told her that she needed me! Yes, I am my own personal advocate as well as my child's.

I pray as you read this book you can use my knowledge and experiences to enrich your life and your family's lives by bringing hope, confidence, information, and a foundation from which you can take back control and be your child's advocate.

Success Stories

For all of you with teenagers, I want you to be inspired by a terrific young man's success!

Hunter's Story (Age 14)

I felt I could not focus in school or on my homework. I was at my very worst. It was frustrating to try to study, see my grades fall and know that it was out of my hands. I had trouble staying awake during the day. I was so tired I was nauseas every morning.

I had been going to my doctor for over two years while they ran at least 20 different blood tests to try to determine why I was so fatigued. I then went to a sleep clinic who thought I had sleep apnea and put me on a CRAP machine, but that didn't work. I went to a sleep neurologist who put me in a sleep study and I wore a monitor for 2 weeks and it showed I did not have sleep apnea or narcolepsy. I felt frustrated that no one could figure out what was wrong with me.

My sleep neurologist suggested that I see a Naturopath to have my Adrenal Gland checked. My mom called Dr. Holland to ask for help and she suggested I take a questionnaire about Candida. After I found out I had Candida, it was a relief! I was finally done going to different doctors. I started the Candida program. I started to feel better and the first time I took a test after I did the program, I did really well on the test! I couldn't believe that I could actually focus on the test. I didn't have to take an entire class over the summer! That was HUGE!

The first day that I felt well was two weeks into the cleanse, right after the 3-day detox, and I had gotten most of the bad stuff out. I was so relieved that "something" was finally working.

The food on the program was very good and it didn't feel like I was on a cleanse at all. Since I found out I have a lot of food allergies, I've had to stay off a lot of foods even after the program. I have my favorite meals and snacks that I like to have and that don't make me sick. I don't mind eating differently because I know it is making me well and healthy. Feeling better is way worth it!

The supplements were easy to take because I would take two pills at a time and I got it out of the way. I also knew that I just wanted to feel better and that was one of the things I had to do.

My football coaches told us to stay away from drive-thrus and don't drink pop. Luckily, I was already doing those things so they were impressed. During football retreat all the players wanted to taste what I was eating because it looked much better than their food. My football coach asked me at every meal what I was eating and then said, "Real men eat rice bread". The cleanse is definitely a challenge and it was tough, but I believe that what doesn't kill you will make you stronger.

For all of you mothers with sick kids, who aren't sure you can make it, this is for you!

Lisa's Story (Hunter's Mother)

Hunter has been sick since he was a toddler. He started having stomach problem in 1st grade. He is now in 10th grade. I remember taking him to a gastroenterologist in 6th grade for severe stomach aches and diarrhea and they diagnosed him with IBS. They gave us no treatment solutions except the advice to eat slower and less amounts. In 7th grade the fatigue started to set in. I took him to his general practitioner who ran tests over the next 2 years with every one coming back "normal". He had countless MRI's and ultrasounds to determine if there was something tangible causing all this discomfort. His only option left was to be tested for a sleep disorder.

After taking him to 2 different sleep clinics, it was determined he was getting plenty of sleep but he felt like he only slept for 3-4 hours every night. In 9th grade the fatigue heightened to the extent that he literally could not get out of bed. As a mom, I felt so helpless and sad to watch him suffer through each morning and each day with no relief of any kind. I never knew if he would be getting up that day or not, so my schedule revolved around his ability to get out of bed. If he did get out of bed, "when" was the next question? How many classes would he miss that day? I remember watching him on the computer trying to work on an assignment when he put his head on the keyboard and said, "I have completely forgotten what I'm doing and I can't live like this anymore". He was forced to drop his first period class due to over 40 absences and no way of catching up. (He will be taking the class on-line in the future to make up for the dropped class.) I would say that we had both hit our bottom when he was asked to leave track practice early and not return to the team because his grades were below the standard. He called me to come pick him up early from practice and when he got in the car I saw tears in his eyes. He loved being in track and was an above average shot put thrower for his age. He would miss districts that next week. I came home that night, sat alone sobbing, and soul searched on where to go from there. That is when Dr. Holland's name popped into my head and I immediately called her to ask for her advice. When she told me she suspected what was wrong with Hunter and that he could get better, I broke down in tears because I couldn't believe that someone finally thought they he could be helped.

When Dr. Holland explained how the program worked to Hunter and I, there was no question in either of our minds that we could do this. As his mom, I knew he would need support by having someone close to him do the program alongside him. After all, he was only 14 at the time. Since I was with him most often, I decided to cleanse my body along with him. We made a pact that as long as we had each other, we could do anything! When Dr. Holland said to think of all the foods you "can" eat instead of all the food you "can't" eat, we grabbed onto the theory and ran with it. We came up with some fairly yummy creations of our own! We had a family meeting and included Hunter's dad and sisters in the "eating" program. They agreed that if this would make Hunter better, then 30 days was no big deal compared to all the years he had been suffering. My 12 year old daughter committed to the program and stuck with it for the 30 days. My husband also ate all the foods we were eating and, although he had started losing weight before the program, he lost a total of 50 pounds! He feels better than he has felt in years.

The hardest part of the program was learning all the foods to avoid and which foods were "legal" to eat. With Dr. Holland's help, we were able to start off with a lot of choices. It was also time consuming to plan our meals for a week at a time so we didn't get in a place where we were hungry with nothing "legal" to eat. The grocery shopping took a lot longer in the beginning because every ingredient matters. Now, it is much easier to shop because we know exactly what brands and types of foods he likes and dislikes and where to get them. The first 3-day detox was very challenging because we were in an environment where there were food vendors surrounding us with the aromas of garlic and kettle corn. If that wasn't enough, we had to watch people eat many foods that we used to eat all the time. Did I forget to tell you how much Hunter loves to eat? From that moment on, we knew that if we could get through that, the rest would be a "piece of cake".

I have learned so much about eating healthier from this program that we no longer have many items in our home that are toxic. My entire family is much more aware of "why"" we eat healthier and make better choices. This program not only made my son better, it made our family closer and more educated on what we put in our mouths.

I am grateful for every day my son gets out of bed, not felling nauseas, and is in the car on time and ready to go work out for his upcoming football season. I wouldn't change anything we had to do to get him better and we would do it again tomorrow if it meant it would improve his quality of life even more. There was never a question in my mind whether to follow the program or not. As a mother, I would do anything it took to see my son healthy, which directly affects his happiness and opportunity for his future. 100% worth every moment!!

chapter one:
Bronson's Story

In March of 1998, we were blessed with a beautiful baby, our first boy, who would be the youngest child in our family. I was excited to be a mother again, especially because I didn't have a clue about what was in store for me over the next few years. I thought I had this "mom thing" down pretty well after helping to raise a 6 year daughter from my husband's first marriage, and having successfully gotten another daughter safely to age 2½. I know many of you are laughing hysterically at this point, but bear with me and my enthusiastic outlook at this juncture in my naive life.

It never occurred to me that the phrase, "It's a boy," would later bring other phrases to mind like, "Pit Bulls are tamer." I was about to embark on the journey of my life! I later learned that being a boy had very little to do with many of the things that we were experiencing together as mother and son. I had never had a boy, or grown up with brothers, so in the beginning, I assumed many of the challenges I faced were "just boy adventures." Not until I starting looking for causes and solutions to our challenges, did I realize that there were many children like mine, and not all boys. In fact, an epidemic was sweeping through our nation capturing our children and exposing them to risks and serious health problems, most of which were avoidable.

At first, I felt extremely guilty for not knowing, what I just didn't know. I also felt guilty that I could have easily protected my family from illness and degenerative disease and I didn't. We can't implement what we don't know. I am here to empathize with you and tell you to leave the past behind. However, after reading this book, you can't say that you don't know better. You will be responsible for implementing new habits and life style changes for your family. You are responsible if you know and you choose not to do anything different.

So here I was with two darling girls and an adorable baby boy, who would only sleep in 20 to 30 minute intervals the entire night. He started fussing all the time and I finally figured out that he cried the hardest right before a bowel movement. Babies generally have great peristaltic action and eat and eliminate on a regular basis, usually like clockwork. My baby boy had the worst diarrhea and screamed every time he was going to eliminate. He had a rash on his bottom and the skin was so raw and sore that it was painful to just look at it. I called the doctor and was told that because I was exclusively breastfeeding that it must be something that I was eating. I immediately started eliminating things from my diet. After about two weeks, I was down to virtually bread and water with no better results. My baby was miserable, so I was miserable, and my family was miserable.

I was the only mom that had a bottle of liquid antacid and a blow dryer on the changing table in the nursery. I was dabbing antacid on my baby's bottom after every diaper change to stop the burning and blow drying him so that he would not be damp. I tried Bag Balm etc. to keep him comfortable. The biggest problem was why he was screaming and why did he have the rash in the first place? What was the cause? I let my mother instinct kick in, and my gut feeling was that he was allergic to my breast milk. That can't happen though, right? Isn't breast milk best? I am here to tell you, not always. In my case, I was actually making my baby sick! I was sick and didn't know it, and was passing it on to my baby. I wouldn't find this out until later. I started to wean him off breast milk and on to formula, but what kind should I use? After several attempts with different brands I saw a small improvement. I was convinced I was on the right path and so I spoke to a neighbor that was a registered nurse and asked for her opinion. She suggested that I try soy formula and that maybe my baby had milk allergies. Bingo! I tried the soy formula for two weeks and saw a drastic improvement. This miserable, sleep deprived, and frustrated mom was at last having some success.

My baby was still a terrible sleeper and he came down with respitory flu at six weeks old. We took him to the emergency room one night when his breathing was labored. They gave us some medicine and told us to use sit in the bathroom with him and let it fill with steam from the shower to ease his breathing. By six months old he had a bright red rash on his face that looked like a wind burn. He was still a horrible sleeper, getting up several times a night. At fourteen months, he started jumping out of the crib and wandering around the house and into our bedroom. I began closing his bedroom door at night. This is when he started to get out of the crib and lay on the floor and pound on the door with his feet. This is not a way anybody wants to be awakened in the night. Boom! Boom! Boom! We padded the door with a blanket. We bought a cool new toddler bed in the shape of a race car. Nothing worked. By now, my immune system was crashing due to sleep deprivation. I was sick often, catching almost every illness coming through the neighborhood.

One night after being awakened by the door pounding for the second time, I had an ingenious thought! I needed to keep my son in his bed at night, and I knew how I would do it! My own mother refers to these as 2:00 a.m. thoughts, and to this day, we will call each other the next morning to share our "2:00 a.m. thoughts." At 7:00 a.m. on a Sunday morning, I drove down to the store and bought a four man tent, one that didn't need stakes to stand upright. I came home and put the race car bed in the playroom and had my husband erect the tent in my son's room. Perfect! I placed a foam pad in the bottom of the tent and placed a sleeping bag, pillow, and my son's favorite blanket inside. I then placed a Fisher Price Cricket lantern and story books in the pockets lining the inside of the tent. Two little camping chairs were placed on the outside of the tent. That night I told my son that he was going camping and we all crawled into the tent. He leaped onto the sleeping bag with his blanket and we read a bed time story, then I crawled out, zipped the tent closed and blew kisses through the screen. He didn't know about opening the zipper on the tent at this point, and so for the first time since birth, we all slept through the night. He was eighteen months old. Over the next few months, the walls of his room were painted with big trees, logs, and wild life, just like the forest. It looked like a real forest campsite!

I became somewhat of a novelty in my neighborhood as local moms would call me to inquire about my son's camping site and specifically the tent. It seems they too had children not sleeping and making mischief at night. I had a greater sense that I was not unique in my problems, just unique in my solutions. I have long been a "fixer," because patience has been a life time challenge of mine. Waiting for solutions to come over time is not my forte, but sometimes God wants us to learn things that will not only strengthen us, but will help us help others. God helps us through others if we will open our hearts and our minds. We have to be teachable. I am writing this book to help strengthen other families by helping you to think about your child's situation from a new perspective.

I wish that I could say that after we erected the indoor campground that everything was smooth sailing. It was not. Around three years old my son developed little bumps all over his body. The bumps started out on his torso and spread to the groin and a few on face. They bumps were raised and were filled with little bits of pus. When we took him to the dermatologist, we were told he had a form of warts that would just go away on their own. They didn't. More patience was required and God was really testing us. I tried wart removers which didn't work. Popping the bumps resulted in them growing back. I started applying the principle of "thinking outside the box," which I will encourage you to do all throughout your life in order to be more efficient in solving and addressing your challenges. I read about rubbing a potato on warts to get them to go away. It couldn't hurt right? We called ours the magic potato. I told my son that this potato had magic powers and would help the bumps go away and we starting rubbing the potato on the warts nightly. We did see a small improvement, but I admit I was disappointed.

It was at this point, God intervened again to teach me a powerful lesson. I believe he could see that I was genuinely applying myself to this problem and needed a little help. He sent one of my sisters to inspire me. This sister called one night and I was telling her about the magic potato. She didn't even laugh. She told me she had just listened to the most incredible story about Dr. Wayne Dyer's daughter, who had the same condition as my son, flat warts. She told me about how they completely rid Dr. Dyer's daughter of the warts. It was no coincidence that we spoke that night. I have since learned that "THERE ARE NO COINCIDENCES!" I now look for purpose in all of the moments in my life. What may be insignificant to me could be life changing for someone else.

After I spoke with my sister that night, I tucked my son into bed. I told him that I had heard a story about a little girl who had the same kind of bumps that he had on his body. I also told him that she was able to get all the bumps to go away. I proceeded to tell him that when I left his room that night, that he needed to go under the covers and talk to the bumps. He should tell the bumps that he didn't need them anymore and that they needed to leave. I told him that if he did this that the bumps would go away, just like they did for the little girl. My son told me he would do this. After I tucked him in and left his room, I stood outside of the door and listened. I could hear him whispering under the covers. I smiled and prayed that this new tactic would work. The next morning the bumps actually looked better. I encouraged him to repeat this ritual each night and by the fourth day all the bumps were gone! This is when I truly understood that the mind had powerful healing capabilities, especially when the mind, body and spirit are all working together towards the same health goal. This was more than a physical healing, it was a spiritual healing.

If we could all have child like faith, we could accomplish grand things that would enrich our lives and those of our fellow man. I recognize that as adults we have become cynical and jaded due to life's lessons and experiences. I also believe that we can step outside of ourselves and self- examine where we can improve our enthusiasm and love for the blessing of just being alive, having an amazing body, which may not be perfect, but is perfect for us.

I learned another powerful life lesson through this experience. God usually helps us through others. We need each other. He humbles us by teaching us to serve others and to open our hearts and minds to unseen possibilities that others, including God, have to offer. Some are unconventional, some simple, and some require an extraordinary amount of faith and dedication. The challenges we receive are what we need at that moment. It is up to us to believe that we can meet the challenge with determination to learn the lesson gifted to us in those trying times of our lives. How will you use this gift to help not only yourself, but others that will cross our paths in quiet moments? Usually, when I have the chance to influence and inspire others, it is in the quiet, easily dismissed moments of my day to day life. I am still working on recognizing more of these moments. In reflection, I have passed by far too many of these moments when I could have been of service to others who needed me. Sometimes I was self absorbed, too busy, or just plain too selfish. I am a work in progress and will remain so until the day I die. However, I vow that I am improving each day and recognize that I can always do a little better.

As we solved one challenge, we tackled another. I was ready to tackle the rash on his face and eczema on his arms and legs. I started reading about the negative effects of sugar on our immune system and skin. This kid was addicted to sugar of every kind. Each morning he was stand at the top of the stairs and yell, "I want hot cocoa!" By this time I had started working with my friend Dr. Nelson at her holistic health care company. I reflected upon the process that I had gone through to get myself well. I thought about the Candida program that I had gone through and realized that my son had Candida. Candida can be transmitted to your child during a vaginal delivery if the mother has Candida. I had it and didn't know it at the time. He was my only vaginal delivery, as my daughter was a C-Section delivery, which probably saved her from getting Candida. Guilt, guilt, and more guilt set in. I gave my baby Candida! "Get over it," I told myself, and help this kid! This is why he was allergic to everything, was a poor sleeper, had diaper rash, bumps and eczema on his skin, had respitory issues, had potty training difficulty, and was addicted to sugar. They were all Candida symptoms and I was just realizing the connection.

If you have overlooked obvious signs in your child, it should give you comfort that I, a professional in integrated health, had difficulty recognizing symptoms in my own child. It is also a lesson that we don't always recognize, or want to admit, that own child has a specific problem or issue. Somehow we think that may reflect negatively on us as the parent, or maybe we are afraid of what that child will have to endure as a result of bringing the problem to the forefront. It can also be scary when we realize that the recognition of the challenge that lies ahead means changes in our own lives. As we accept and face these challenges, we can bless the lives of family, friends, and strangers that we have yet to meet.

When I had this moment of enlightenment, I immediately decided that the entire family would go on a Candida program. I had never worked with anyone who had detoxed a three year old child. I had never detoxed a three year old child, but I knew that this was the road forward. Detoxing was a small part of the program. The significant impact on his health would be the very strict Candida eating regiment and supplementation that was essential to getting healthy and staying well. I knew what I had to do for my son and nothing could keep me from helping him achieve wellness. I was well, my son became well and you and your children can become well also.

chapter two:
What is Candida?

Candida is an over-infestation of yeast in the body. When too much yeast exists in the body, it invades every tissue of the body including the brain. Candida grows and lives on what you eat and makes you crave what it thrives on. Candida may occur alone or in combination with any autoimmune disorder, which includes being over weight, which I consider an autoimmune disorder. There are medical tests for yeast, including stool sample testing. However, symptom screening is a very effective, low cost, non-invasive way to test for Candida. Individuals who do not have Candida will not relate to the questions being asked, while Candida sufferers generally score quite high on the test. Candida can be transmitted through sexual contact, pregnancy, or common area tubs. Just say no to sitting in a public hot tub potentially full of yeast and fungus. Gross!

Self Test for Candida
YES NO
- ❏ ❏ Do you suffer from intestinal gas, abdominal bloating or discomfort?
- ❏ ❏ Do you crave sugar, breads, beer, or alcoholic beverages?
- ❏ ❏ Are you bothered by bowel disorders, constipation, diarrhea, or both?
- ❏ ❏ Do you suffer from anxiety, depression, panic attacks or mood swings?
- ❏ ❏ Are you often irritable, easily angered anxious or nervous?
- ❏ ❏ Do you have trouble thinking clearly or suffer memory loss?
- ❏ ❏ Are you ever faint, feel dizzy or light-headed?
- ❏ ❏ Do you have muscle aches or take more than 24 hours to recover from normal activity?
- ❏ ❏ Without a change in diet, have you had weight gain and not been able to lose the weight no matter what you have tried?
- ❏ ❏ Does itching or burning of the vagina, rectum or prostate bother you, or have you experienced a loss of sexual desire?
- ❏ ❏ Do you have white or yellow fuzzy coating on your tongue?
- ❏ ❏ Have you had athlete's foot, ringworm, jock itch or other chronic fungus infection of the skin or nails?

❏ ❏ Does exposure to perfumes, insecticides, new carpeting, or other chemical smells bother you?
❏ ❏ Have you at any time in your life taken "broad spectrum" antibiotics?
❏ ❏ Are you using birth control pills or shots, or have you done so at any time in your life?
❏ ❏ Are you on synthetic hormones?
❏ ❏ Have you ever taken steroid drugs?

Rate Your Results

"Yes" Answers	Probability of a yeast problem
12 or more	Very High
7 to 11	High
5 to 6	Moderate
0 to 4	Low at this time

Everybody has yeast and friendly bacteria in their body. We don't start calling the yeast Candida until there is an overabundance in the body. This happens we destroy the friendly bacteria in the body that is keeping the yeast in check. What things in your diet, lifestyle, and environment make you susceptible to getting Candida?

Antibiotics kill not only the bad, but also the good bacteria in the body (this includes the antibiotics in meat and dairy products that we consume each day). Even one dose can kill all friendly bacteria.

- Steroid Drugs – cortisones, birth control pills, laxatives.
- Alcohol – destroys enzymes and lacto bacteria.
- Coffee destroys friendly bacteria.
- Stress
- Aging
- Anything that weakens the immune system also affects the balance of beneficial and harmful bacteria.
- Sugar – any foods containing white sugars and sugar substitutes.
- Gluten – any foods that contain gluten; breads, pastries, etc.
- Meat – feeds the bacillus coli (harmful bacteria) which then overruns the friendly bacteria.
- Any foods that use fermentation, molds or vinegars in the production process.

Candida symptoms take on many forms depending on gender, age, and longevity of the active Candida in the system. It can also depend on the immune system state at the time of onset. There are many common symptoms that can be present at individual times or simultaneously. Symptoms may include, but are not limited to:

- Allergic reaction; congestion, hives, headache, dizziness, diarrhea, weakness, cramps, arthritis, irritability, depression, increased sensitivities.
- Gastrointestinal problems
- Respiratory problems
- Cardiovascular problems; (Candida does not directly effect heart, but rather the hormones regulating the system.)
- Genitourinary problems; yeast infections, urinary burning, frequent urination, lack of bladder control, bed wetting, menstrual cramping, PMS.
- Musculoskeletal problems; muscle weakness, night leg pains, muscle stiffness, (especially neck and shoulder) slow reaction time, poor coordination, poor motor skills, falling, tendency to drop things. (Yeast impairs cells from receiving nutrients and eliminating waste and also nerve/muscle sending patterns.)
- Skin infections usually rash type in nature, typically under the breasts, groin area, diaper rash, hives, etc.
- Central nervous system problems; headache, sinus headache, tension headache, migraines, low blood sugar headaches, rapid blood sugar changes.
- High levels of stress hormones can cause anxiety, irritability, restlessness, panic attacks, sudden anger, sleep disturbances, poor short term memory, inability to concentrate, confusion.
- Fatigue may be caused by impaired metabolism and impaired enzyme production.
- Weight gain may result from an overgrowth of yeast which may cause cravings for sugar, interference with normal hunger, high insulin levels, low metabolism, low energy levels, and fatigue.

Can I get a prescription for the yeast? Yes you can, if you want to keep having yeast problems for the rest of your life! It sounds fun doesn't it? Conventional medicine, if they even acknowledge that you have Candida, will prescribe medication that will drive the yeast into the connective tissues and into a dormant state where it lies in wait. A common scenario is to have finished a course of antibiotics or steroid drugs and shortly thereafter end up with a yeast infection. Drugs that specifically address the fungus or Candida destroy some of the yeast. The yeasts that are not affected by the drugs begin to colonize in vast numbers and become more drug-resistant. As the yeast multiplies in its stronger state, they produce toxins that attack the body's defense. These same drugs also destroy the friendly bacteria in the body so there is no defense against the new, stronger strains.

The Holistic Approach to Treating Candida

Detoxification

Yeast Control Formula/Friendly Bacteria)

100% Nutrition *(You must use supplements to achieve this)*

Water

Exercise

A yeast control diet *(The most crucial part, and the most strict)*

In order to achieve harmony in the body and bring the yeast and friendly bacteria levels back to an acceptable level, the yeast must be starved to death and then immediately flushed from the body. At the same time this is happening, 100% nutrition should be supplied to the body through Non-Candida foods and supplementation that replaces friendly bacteria, a multi-vitamin/mineral supplement, and omega 3, 6 and 9 fatty acids.

I recommend using a very strict program that provides support and guidance through a well outlined daily calendar. By following a very strict protocol, most people are symptom free in 30 days. A small population of my clients goes through 60 days of program. Generally these are very severe cases, or clients that have not adhered to the strict rules the first 30 days. Save yourself a lot of frustration, expense, and drama by just committing to 30 days of the Candida program right up front. You and your child will be greatly rewarded with the results.

Contrary to other information that may be out there, Candida can NOT be solved by just taking supplement or prescription drugs. I could give you supplements all day long and unless you and your child adhere to the strict eating regiment, you will never get well. At this junction in the consultation my clients feel a little overwhelmed and nervous about how to accomplish becoming symptom free. Some, however, feel relieved that somebody finally understands what is wrong and will provide step by step instruction on how to become well again.

When I was sick, and when my child was sick, I used the M'lis Candida program to help us get well. This is the program that I have been recommending for ten years. I recommend it because it works. I spent many years examining different approaches to treating Candida, and I believe that this one is the best. It is the best because it incorporates the eating regiment, supplements, exercise, and hydration on an easy to follow 30 calendar designed for Candida and fungus. In ten years, I have not ever had a client who has strictly followed the program, who has not gotten well. The program is that good!

You may call the M'lis Company if you are interested in using their supplements, the products listed on the program calendar. They can refer you to a retail outlet near you. Their number is 800-548-0569. If you are unable to locate a health spa or medical clinic near you which sells the M'lis supplements, please adhere to the following guidelines.

Supplements should be in a veggie capsule (next best is a gelatin capsule). NO PRESS TABS! (They do not break down enough in the body to provide nutrition or support!)

Supplements can NOT contain any yeast, sugar, gluten, corn or artificial flavoring or colors.

Try to get supplements from a company where the products are designed to work in harmony with one another. When you buy different brands, sometimes the quality and strength of the supplements won't create the needed balance we are striving for on the program.

Look for supplements with very little or no fillers. This is difficult to check as supplements are not FDA regulated in the United States. Many of the inexpensive brands use a lot of filler material in their supplements to drive the cost down. *Testing products by using a glass of water to watch dissolving time is not a good way to verify a quality product. For instance, the M'lis brand products are designed to digest with the digestive enzymes produced by the body, or digestive enzyme supplements, not water. Your body uses enzymes to help absorb the nutrients from the supplements and foods you eat.

I usually recommend families start with the Candida program, as I believe it is the most direct and helpful way to begin regaining your health. I also believe that the majority of families who have poor health have some degree of over-infestation of yeast in the body. I have discovered that nearly all of the individuals, who have auto-immune disorders, also have Candida. I have also discovered that some individuals who have been told they have an auto-immune disorder, like Fibromyalgia, really have Candida. In summary, it's just a great program to gaining back control of your health in the most timely and thorough manner.

When your family starts this program you will all be eating the same recommended foods while avoiding the foods not permitted.

Children, or small adults, that weigh less than 100 lbs., should take half of the dosage outlined on the M'lis Calendar.

The child needs to detoxify with the rest of the family or family support person, who is doing the program with them.

Make this a fun time. You can have a reward or small prize for your child when they complete the detoxification days, with little or no complaining.

Have activities planned that will keep you and your child busy and not thinking about food during the detoxification days.

You can open some of the powdered capsules and mix the supplements in the MRP shake or other foods like oatmeal to disguise it. The M'lis MRP shake tastes like a real treat without any sugar or Candida feeding ingredients, this is a great way to get in the supplements if you have to open the capsules for your child's consumption. The chocolate is one of my client's favorite for supplement disguising!

Be prepared. Make a menu for one week of Candida approved foods and rotate through that menu for a month. You may be sick of some of the foods by the end of the program, however, you will be less stressed and you enjoy what you are eating.

Clean out that refrigerator, freezer and all of your cupboards, desk drawers, and even your purse. Any place that you may have foods that would ruin your program should be thrown away, donated or boxed up. You may mindlessly munch on food that is not approved for your program and have to start all over.

Keep it simple! Don't make different meals for family members not on the program. The Candida program foods are wonderful and healthy and everyone can enjoy eating them. Do not cater to other family member's bad habits. Lovingly explain that you have prepared a tasty meal for the whole family. Any complainers can make their own food or go without. Nobody is going to starve to death!

Your child may whine and cry, but as a good parent you know that it is just a ploy to get you to give in to toxic foods or take them off program. Yes, you and your child may experience a healing crisis on the program, most likely you will. This is just part of the healing process by working through your past health history. It is also true that your child's complaint is probably legitimate if they tell you that they don't feel well, especially during detoxification days. Make sure that you keep yourself and your child hydrated and your blood sugar levels regulated. Rest if you need to and otherwise stay busy to keep your mind occupied.

You are your child's advocate! Stay the course and be consistent. 30 days of mild discomfort is nothing compared to a life time of poor health. If you usually give into your child's whims and whines then get somebody else in your family to do the program with your child, you can't afford to be weak. Your child's health is at risk.

If you have access to a body composition machine, monitor you and your child's hydration levels, body fat, lean muscle mass, weight, and kcal reading so that you can get excited about what is happening on the inside of your amazing body. The changes on the inside will often be noticeable before the outward appearance changes. It is a life changing journey.

Make sure that you and your child are eating regularly. If possible, 5 to 6 small meals a day to keep the blood sugar levels regulated and metabolism up. I use the bottom shelf of a cupboard and the bottom shelf of my refrigerator for my kid's snacks. I recommend pre-bagging vegetables, olives, Candida friendly crackers and chips, and other approved program snacks. You and your child will be much more comfortable knowing that your program food is ready and waiting. Always have some of these snack bags with you and your child so that you don't get into a situation where you need to eat and no appropriate food is available.

Keep a wellness journal every day to track what is happening with you and your child on the program. This is not optional. This will help your program mentor, if you have one, and also you, to see where you need to improve or if you are following the program as outlined. The journal should list ALL daily food intake, water consumption, exercise and stress relieving techniques. You may also choose to briefly write about how you are feeling that day as it can be tied to certain foods, or hormonal changes. This is invaluable information for monitoring your success.

Have a happy positive attitude. Know that you will be successful. This is more important than anything else in your program. This program is a gift and should be viewed as the valuable treasure that it is. You will be well.

REMEMBER: *You can't cheat even one time on this program. Candida is a living organism that lives off of what you feed it and it also makes you crave what it lives on. You feed it, you start over on day number one!*

Here is the M'lis program I use when helping families eliminate Candida and fungus problems from the body:

What You CAN Eat on the Candida Program

- All fish, poultry, turkey, rabbit, water packed tuna, and eggs.
- All vegetables. (no corn)
- All legumes and beans
- All whole wheat muffins, biscuits tortillas, rice cakes. (no yeast)
- Hot or cold cereals: Wheatena, grits, Oat Bran, Shredded Wheat, Puffed Rice, Zoom, Oatmeal, Wheat Hearts, Puffed Wheat Roman Meal, or Cracked Wheat.
- Unprocessed nuts and seeds-except peanuts and pistachios.
- Butter and cold pressed oils such as walnut, linseed, olive, sunflower, and safflower.
- Unsweetened Soy, Rice or Almond Milk, plain unsweetened yogurt, ricotta cheese (no vinegar), cottage cheese, plain cream cheese, unsweetened tofu. (WATCH OUT FOR RICE SYRUPS AND CANE JUICE)
- Use of miso or soy sauce sparingly.
- 100% vegetable glycerin or stevia for sweetening, M'lis Simply Sweet and 100% Pure Maple Syrup after day 11.
- Lemon/Lime

Food NOT Permitted During the Candida Program

YOU MUST READ THE LABELS ON EVERYTHING

Items underlined on the list, should not be reintroduced even when wellness has been achieved, or should be eaten in extreme moderation.

- <u>Red meat and pork</u>
- <u>All sugar and sugar-containing food</u> including: Table sugar, corn syrup, honey, molasses, maple sugar, date sugar, rice syrups, maltodextrin, and cane juice. *(If the item ends in OSE, this tells you that it is a sugar.)*
- Fructose
- <u>All white flour and white flour product</u>. <u>All yeast containing products</u>.
- Brewers yeast, B vitamins made from yeast, yeast breads, pastries
- <u>All cheese, including hard cheeses.</u>
- <u>No alcoholic beverages</u>
- No fruit juices or fruits until yeast is abated.

- No coffee or tea
- Herbal teas. *(Use hot water and lemon and/or ginger root with Simply Sweet or Stevia if you need a hot drink.)*
- No leftovers older that 3 days. Leftovers may be frozen.
- Obvious fungus foods: mushrooms, blue cheese, etc.
- Peanuts, and peanut products, pistachios.
- All processed meats: bacon, sausage, ham, hot dogs,
- Lunch meats. *(You can buy a plain turkey breast to cook, and cut it up for sandwiches. There are a few pre-cooked turkey breasts which are o.k. for program)*
- All vinegar-soaked products or vinegar dressings: pickles, pickle relish. *(Annie's brand has a couple of dressings that are vinegar and sugar free; otherwise just use olive oil and lemon.)*
- Artificially sweetened drinks and food products (Aspartame, Splenda, Nutra-Sweet, Sweet and Low). This means that all gum and breath mints are off limits until you are finished with the program.
- Dairy products: milk, buttermilk, whipped cream, sour cream, ice cream.
- Corn (fresh, canned, frozen)

Sample Candida Meal Plan (be creative)

First Week

DAY 1
Breakfast: Candida-friendly cereal, unsweetened soy milk
Lunch: Veggie salad, with broiled chicken strips
Dinner: Fish, steamed asparagus

DAY 2
Breakfast: Plain unsweetened yogurt with oats, carrot juice
Lunch: Veggie scramble
Dinner: Teriyaki chicken, green beans (marinate in soy sauce and ginger)

DAY 3
Breakfast: Candida-friendly pancakes
Lunch: Chicken salad
Dinner: Duck, spinach

DAY 4
Breakfast: Oatmeal (no sugar)
Lunch: Tuna sandwich
Dinner: Vegetable pasta with Candida-friendly tomato sauce

DAY 5
Breakfast: Eggs, hashed brown potatoes
Lunch: Romaine salad with cottage cheese and baby tomatoes
Dinner: Chicken and brown rice

DAY 6
Breakfast: Biscuit with cream cheese
Lunch: Tuna salad
Dinner: Turkey, beets, and potatoes

DAY 7
Breakfast: Plain unsweetened yogurt with lemons or limes
Lunch: Green salad
Dinner: Veggie stir-fry

DAY 8
Breakfast: Oatmeal
Lunch: Barley soup
Dinner: Veggie lasagna, steamed broccoli

Second Week

DAYS 9, 10, AND 11
Detoxify: Mixture of distilled water, lemon and pure maple syrup

DAY 12
Breakfast: Cucumbers
Lunch: Salad (fresh veggies only)
Dinner: More salad (fresh veggies only)

DAY 13
Breakfast: Oatmeal (yea you can put maple syrup in it!)
Lunch: Veggie stir-fry
Dinner: Spinach salad with olive oil, squash (add maple syrup for sweetness)

DAY 14
Breakfast: Candida-friendly cereal
Lunch: Tuna salad
Dinner: Chili

DAY 15
Breakfast: Eggs and Candida-friendly toast
Lunch: Ricotta cheese tortilla wrap
Dinner: Chicken pot pie

Third Week

DAY 16
Breakfast: Muffins with cooked fruit
Lunch: Rolled chicken tacos
Dinner: Baked potato and a salad with cottage cheese

DAY 17
Breakfast: Oatmeal
Lunch: Salad
Dinner: Veggie stir-fry

DAY 18
Breakfast: Biscuits and cream cheese
Lunch: Chicken salad
Dinner: Ricotta or cottage cheese stuffed pasta shells with homemade tomato sauce

DAY 19
Breakfast: Candida-friendly cereal
Lunch: Tuna sandwich
Dinner: Brown rice and veggie scramble

DAY 20
Breakfast: Almonds and plain unsweetened yogurt
Lunch: Spinach salad
Dinner: Chicken taco's

DAY21
Breakfast: Muffins with cooked fruit
Lunch: Chicken sandwich
Dinner: Duck and broccoli

DAY 22
Breakfast: Yogurt with cooked fruit
Lunch: Tuna salad
Dinner: Salmon and asparagus

Fourth Week

DAY 23
Breakfast: Whole grain french toast
Lunch: Green salad with sliced almonds
Dinner: Chicken and brown rice

DAY 24
Breakfast: Bran muffins and a banana
Lunch: Turkey sandwich
Dinner: Chicken and veggie stir-fry

DAY 25
Breakfast: Yogurt with oats
Lunch: Green salad with raspberries
Dinner: Spinach lasagna

DAY 26
Breakfast: Candida-friendly cereal
Lunch: Brown rice and spinach
Dinner: Chicken soft shell taco

DAY 27
Breakfast: Yogurt with fruit
Lunch: Chicken sandwich
Dinner: Chicken and potatoes

DAY 28
Breakfast: Oatmeal with peaches
Lunch: Tuna salad
Dinner: Salad

DAY 29
Breakfast: Eggs and toast
Lunch: Baked potato
Dinner: Chicken soft shell taco

DAY 30

Breakfast: Fruit
Lunch: Turkey sandwich
Dinner: Salad and fruit

Snack ideas: Yeast-free bran muffins, celery and almond butter, Candida-friendly crackers or chips, baby carrots, oats, hummus, raw nuts and seeds, cream cheese, cottage cheese, olives (no vinegar), salsa (no sugar or vinegar)

Drink at least two quarts of water per day, or a better guide would be to drink half your body weight in ounces. Example: If you weigh 150 lbs, you would drink 75 oz. of water a day.

Remember, you can do anything for 30 days. If you are not willing to dedicate at least 30 to 60 days for you and/or your child to be healthy, you should stop reading this book and come back to it when your family is sick and tired of being sick and tired. It's up to you! Your fairy godmother is not coming!

The M'lis Candida Program Calendar: First Month

THE M'LIS CANDIDA PROGRAM - MONTH 1

DAY	1	2	3	4	5	6	7	8	9	10
DATE										
INSTRUCTIONS	2 qts water; eliminate red meat, dairy, fruit, refined sugars & flours; eat whole grains (no yeast), fresh veggies & their juice	continue as day before Candida Combo, Detox. Group #1	continue as day before exercise 30 min.	continue as day before	continue as day before exercise 30 min.	continue as day before	continue as day before eliminate all meat exercise 30 min.	continue as day before	**DETOXIFY** Detox. Group #1 Probiotic-Herb	**DETOXIFY** Detox. Group #2 Probiotic-Herb exercise 30 min.

DAY	11	12	13	14	15	16	17	18	19	20
DATE										
INSTRUCTIONS	**DETOXIFY** Detox. Group #3 Probiotic-Herb continue up to 10 days	eat fresh veggies, Wrap & Massage exercise 30 min.	continue as day before add whole grains (no yeast)	continue as day before add lean protein exercise 30 min. add steamed veggies	continue as day before add "legal" dairy	continue as day before	continue as day before	continue as day before	continue as day before exercise 30 min.	continue as day before

take Candida Combo & Detox. Group #1

DAY	21	22	23	24	25	26	27	28	29	30
DATE										
INSTRUCTIONS	continue as day before exercise 30 min. Wrap & Massage	continue as day before	continue as day before	continue as day before exercise 30 min.	continue as day before	continue as day before	continue as day before	continue as day before exercise 30 min.	continue as day before	continue as day before exercise 30 min.

CANDIDA COMBINATION

SUPPLEMENT	AM	NOON	PM
CALCIUM	2		2
PROBIOTIC	2-2		2-2
DAILY	1		1
EVENING PRIMROSE OIL	2		2
FLAX SEED OIL	3		3
TRANQUILITY	2		2
VITAL	1		
VITAMIN D	2		2
ENZYME	Take 2 with each meal, or with M'lis Instant Meal		
INSTANT MEAL	Drink up to 2x daily		
MAINTAIN	Use following every bath or shower to help cleanse connective tissue		
SLENDER AID	Take 2 as often as necessary (up to 3x/day) to appease appetite and regulate blood sugar		

DETOXIFICATION HERBS - GROUP 1

HERBS	AM	PM
CLEANSE	2	2
DETOX	2	2
FIBER	8	8

DETOXIFICATION HERBS - GROUP 2

HERBS	AM	PM
CLEANSE	2	2
DETOX	3	3
FIBER	8	8

DETOXIFICATION HERBS - GROUP 3

HERBS	AM	PM
CLEANSE	2	2
DETOX	4	4
FIBER	8	8

Exercise as listed above, or if possible, for a minimum of 20-30 minutes 5 times/week, and drink at least 8 glasses of water daily. To maintain wellness, continue to provide the body with 100% nutrition with M'lis DAILY and CALCIUM supplements, along with a well balanced diet. M'lis recommends DETOXIFICATION 3-4 times each year for overall health.

by JulieAnn Holland, Ph.D.

The M'lis Candida Program Calendar: Second Month

THE M'LIS CANDIDA PROGRAM - MONTH 2

DAY	1	2	3	4	5	6	7	8	9	10
DATE										
INSTRUCTIONS	2 qts. water; eliminate red meat, dairy, fruit, refined sugars & flours; eat whole grains (no yeast), fresh veggies & their juice	continue as day before Candida Combo. Detox. Group #1	continue as day before exercise 30 min.	continue as day before	continue as day before exercise 30 min.	continue as day before	continue as day before eliminate all meat exercise 30 min.	continue as day before	DETOXIFY Detox. Group #1 Probiotic Herb	DETOXIFY Detox. Group #2 Probiotic Herb exercise 30 min.

DAY	11	12	13	14	15	16	17	18	19	20
DATE										
INSTRUCTIONS	DETOXIFY Detox. Group #3 Probiotic Herb continue up to 30 days	eat fresh veggies, Wrap & Massage exercise 30 min.	continue as day before add whole grains (no yeast)	continue as day before add lean protein exercise 30 min. add steamed veggies	continue as day before add "legal" daily	continue as day before may add cooked fruit to recipes	continue as day before	continue as day before	continue as day before exercise 30 min.	continue as before

take Candida Combo. & Detox. Group #1

DAY	21	22	23	24	25	26	27	28	29	30
DATE										
INSTRUCTIONS	continue as day before exercise 30 min. Wrap & Massage	continue as day before gradually add whole grain yeast bread & fresh fruit one at a time	continue as day before	continue as day before	continue as day before	continue as day before exercise 30 min.	continue as day before	continue as day before exercise 30 min.	continue as day before	continue as day before exercise 30 min.

DETOX - see notes below if not continuing on with another M'lis program.

CANDIDA COMBINATION

SUPPLEMENT	AM	NOON	PM
CALCIUM	2		2
PROBIOTIC	2-2		2-2
DAILY	1		1
EVENING PRIMROSE OIL	2		2
FLAX SEED OIL	3		3
TRANQUILITY	2		2
VITAL	1		
VITAMIN D	2		2
ENZYME	Take 2 with each meal, or with M'lis Instant Meal		
INSTANT MEAL	Drink up to 2x daily		
MAINTAIN	Use following every bath or shower to help cleanse connective tissue		
SLENDER AID	Take 2 as often as necessary (up to 3x/day) to appease appetite and regulate blood sugar		

DETOXIFICATION HERBS - GROUP 1

HERBS	AM	PM
CLEANSE	2	2
DETOX	2	2
FIBER	8	8

DETOXIFICATION HERBS - GROUP 2

HERBS	AM	PM
CLEANSE	2	2
DETOX	3	3
FIBER	8	8

DETOXIFICATION HERBS - GROUP 3

HERBS	AM	PM
CLEANSE	2	2
DETOX	4	4
FIBER	8	8

Drink at least 1/2 your body's weight in ounces of water daily. If this program is not followed by another M'lis program, detoxify at end of candida program. On day 26 & 27, follow the instructions for day 7; then detoxify on days 28, 29 and 30. Exercise as listed above, for a minimum of 20-30 minutes 5 times/week, and drink at least 8 glasses of water daily. To maintain wellness, continue to provide the body with 100% nutrition with M'lis DAILY and CALCIUM supplements, along with a well balanced diet. M'lis recommends DETOXIFICATION 3-4 times each year for overall health.

I Am My Child's Advocate

chapter three:
Earning Your Health, Good, Bad, and Really Bad

I am constantly amazed at how naive families can be about how much personal lifestyle has a direct and significant impact on health. In today's world with daily health segments on TV, the internet, magazines and newspapers, reporting on the affects of food dyes, chemicals, lack of exercise and medication side effects etc., a family would have to be a virtual hermit and living a very sheltered life to not hear about lifestyle choices affecting health. Even our government, as misguided and damaging as many of their efforts are, has programs in the school system to educate children about healthier habits. Granted, a small majority really might not know, or just might not get it However, I believe that our society has become intrinsically lazy. I know that is what happened to me. We want what's quick and easy because our lives have become dependant on instant gratification. I also admit that a lot of that "garbage" they call food does taste really good! I also know that if our life is filled with "garbage" eventually we will feel just like "garbage"!

It is a wonder that we believe that we can basically eat a diet of almost all dead things and expect to feel alive and wonderful. I was first introduced to the concept of eating mostly all live foods when I was suffering form Fibromyalgia. After I rid my body of the Candida, I was able to implement a diet of juicing and raw foods to eliminate my Fibromyalgia symptoms. It was difficult and so much work! The healing crisis was intense. I broke out in sores all over the inside of my mouth. I had boils on my skin and a severe case of diarrhea! Disgusting! One day I just broke down and cried because I thought, "How can this be making me well? I feel awful!" However, I stuck it out, having tried almost everything else. I soon began to get relief in my poor aching body. In those first few weeks I really had to examine my symptoms and look past the entire healing crisis in order to buoy my spirits so that I could stay steadfast in my new eating regiment. Did I mention that all the vegetables that I was juicing made me gag? They did!

Being sick and tired is ten times worse than juicing every two hours. Looking back I am grateful for my stubborn nature that enabled me to want to crush Fibromyalgia and all of the symptoms that accompany this vicious disorder. Yes, I earned the health that I have by what I did and did not do with my lifestyle choices. So what did I learn from this experience that helped my family and increased my conviction to be my child's advocate? Live food is essential to life, a life worth living. Each meal at our house has live food on the table. My children have learned that I expect them to eat live food at every meal, even in their lunches that I pack each day. Live food is power food.

There is mounting research that reveals that the quality of nutrients we put into our bodies determines the quality of our lives. If you had an expensive sports car with a high performance engine, what kind of fuel would you put into your car for optimal performance? Depending upon the quality of the fuel used, the longevity and performance of the car is greatly affected. We must all realize that food quality directly determines our physical and mental performance now and in especially in the future. Maybe you can buy a new car, but you must earn good health.

Wild animals are never obese, only human beings and domesticated animals (due to human influence). I have a colleague and friend, who has been advocating a pre-World Word II diet for many years. She said that this is the way that we need to go back to eating in order to get healthy again. What is so great about the diet and the eating habits of our ancestors? Prior to the 1950s, many of the "common" diseases and disorders that inflict us today were virtually nonexistent. The human race is the only species that experiences the problem of obesity and has degenerative disease as a primary cause of death.

Degenerative Diseases Not Known Of or Diagnosed Before 1950

- **Diabetes & Hypoglycemia** (blood sugar disorders)
  150 million Americans suffer from these disorders (most common in adults over 45 with a sedentary lifestyle)

- **Alzheimer's & Dementia** (low to no memory function)
  40 million Americans suffer from these disorders

- **Hypothyroidism and Hyperthyroidism** (thyroid disorders)
  10 million Americans suffer from hypothyroidism while 5 million Americans suffer from hyperthyroidism

- **High Blood Pressure**
  As many as 25% of American adults suffer from high blood pressure

- **High Cholesterol**
  Most Americans suffer from high cholesterol—#1 risk factor for heart disease aside from smoking

- **Fibromyalgia**
  20 million Americans suffer from this disease

- **Candida** (an over-infestation of yeast)
  50% of everyone screened for this disorder
- **Hormonal Imbalances**
  50% of everyone screened show up with hormonal imbalances
- **Heart Disease**
  #1 leading cause of death among American adults. More than 23.5 million Americans suffer from some form of heart disease.
- **Multiple Sclerosis**
  More than 350,000 Americans diagnosed
- **Depression & Anxiety**
  9.5% of U.S. population or 18.8 million Americans suffer from some sort of anxiety or depression
- **Arthritis**
  66 million Americans suffer from some form of arthritis
- **Osteoporosis**
  10 million Americans suffer from osteoporosis while 18 million more have lost some bone mass
- **Lupus**
  1.5 million Americans suffer from lupus
- **Parkinson's Disease**
  In the U.S. it is believed that nearly 500,000 people suffer from Parkinson's Disease

The evidence is overwhelming in favor of lifestyle being a major component in our health, the health that we earn with each and every choice that we make. We can do better, a lot better. We can change the future of health for upcoming generations by our example in our own homes, offices and schools.

I realize that we live in a real world of stress and chaos and it may not be realistic to eat raw foods all day every day. I expect my clients, who have diseases and disorders that need immediate attention and relief to be more extreme. I have practiced using this way of eating for the last ten years, and I can testify that it really does work. When you get off track you can really see a difference in your health. When we start making small steps towards eating better each day, we will one day realize that great things have been accomplished. If you or your child is very sick, I would encourage you to commit to a strict and structured program that I will outline. Remember that live foods are healing foods.

If you suspect you have Candida, you MUST complete a Candida program first, or you will never get well. The immune system boosting program has many healthy foods that will feed yeast if there is already an over-infestation in the body. Once you have completed the Candida program, any remaining symptoms can be addressed with the immune system program. The immune system program consists of primarily live foods, most of which are juiced every two hours.

M'lis Immune System Recovery Calendar

M'LIS IMMUNE SYSTEM RECOVERY PROGRAM - MONTH 1

DAY	1	2	3	4	5	6	7	8	9	10
DATE										
INSTRUCTIONS	eliminate meat, dairy, refined sugars & flours Immune Combo. Detox. Group #1	eliminate meat, dairy, refined sugars & flours Immune Combo. Detox. Group #1	DETOXIFY Detox. Group #1 Use Maintain Lotion as directed below	DETOXIFY Detox. Group #2 Continue use of Maintain Lotion	DETOXIFY Detox. Group #3 Continue use of Maintain Lotion	15 min. walk. fresh juice every 2 hrs. Immune Combo. Detox. Group #1 Therapeutic Wrap & Massage	15 min. walk. fresh juice every 2 hrs. Immune Combo. Detox. Group #1	fresh juice every 2 hrs. Immune Combo. Detox. Group #1	20 min. walk. fresh juice every 2 hrs. Immune Combo. Detox. Group #1	fresh juice every 2 hrs. fresh fruit & vegetables Immune Combo. Detox. Group #1

DAY	11	12	13	14	15	16	17	18	19	20
DATE										
INSTRUCTIONS	continue as day before 20 min. walk, add yogurt, whole grains	continue as day before 10 min. walk add lean proteins	continue as day before 20 min. walk add nuts & seeds	continue as day before 20 min. walk add steamed veggies	continue as day before 30 min. walk	continue as day before Therapeutic Wrap & Massage	continue as day before 30 min. walk	continue as day before 10 min. walk	continue as day before 10 min. walk	continue as day before 30 min. walk

DAY	21	22	23	24	25	26	27	28	29	30
DATE										
INSTRUCTIONS	continue as day before 10 min. walk	continue as day before 30 min. walk	continue as day before 30 min. walk	continue as day before 10 min. walk	DETOXIFY Detox. Group #1 Use Maintain Lotion	DETOXIFY Detox. Group #2 Use Maintain Lotion	DETOXIFY Detox. Group #3 Use Maintain Lotion	fresh juice every 2 hrs. Immune Combo. Detox. Group #1 Therapeutic Wrap & Massage	15 min. walk. fresh juice every 2 hrs. Immune Combo. Detox. Group #1	20 min. walk. fresh juice every 2 hrs. Immune Combo. Detox. Group #1

continue rotation of fresh juices, fruits and vegetables, as well as yogurt, whole grains, lean proteins

rotate fresh juices, fruits and vegetables, as well as yogurt, whole grains, and lean proteins - digest something every 2 hours

IMMUNE SYSTEM RECOVERY COMBINATION

HERB	AM	NOON	PM
CALCIUM	2		2
DAILY	1		1
DHEA	1		
EVENING PRIMROSE OIL	2		2
FLAX SEED OIL	3		3
RELIEF	3	3	3
TRANQUILITY	2		2
VITAL	1		
VITAMIN D	2	1	2
ENZYME	Take 2 with each meal, or with M'lis Instant Meal		
INSTANT MEAL	Drink up to 2x daily		
MAINTAIN	Use daily on sore muscles & joints following every bath or shower		
SLENDER AID	Take 2 as often as necessary (up to 3x/day) to appease appetite and regulate blood sugar		

DETOXIFICATION HERBS - GROUP 1

HERBS	AM	PM
CLEANSE	2	2
DETOX	2	3
FIBER	8	8

DETOXIFICATION HERBS - GROUP 2

HERBS	AM	PM
CLEANSE	2	2
DETOX	3	3
FIBER	8	8

DETOXIFICATION HERBS - GROUP 3

HERBS	AM	PM
CLEANSE	2	2
DETOX	4	4
FIBER	8	8

*M'lis recommends the purchase of a "Juice Book". Rotate juice recipes often for variation in diet. Exercise as listed above, or if possible, for a minimum of 20-30 minutes 5 times/week, and drink 1/2 your body's weight in ounces of water daily. To maintain wellness, continue to provide the body with 100% nutrition with M'lis DAILY and CALCIUM supplements, along with a well balanced diet. M'lis recommends DETOXIFICATION 3-4 times each year for overall health.

Common Immune System Disorders Improved by the Immune System Recovery Program:

- Multiple Sclerosis
- Lupus
- Fibromyalgia
- Overweight or Obesity
- Hashimoto's Disease
- Scleroderma
- Juvenile Rheumatoid Arthritis
- HIV and AIDS
- Asthma
- Allergies
- Eczema and Psoriasis
- Reynaud's Disease
- Diabetes
- IBS
- Chrones Disease
- Colitis and Diverticulitis

Summary of Juicing Basics

- Extracted from fresh, raw fruits and vegetables.
- These are digested in minutes instead of hours.
- Fruits provide carbohydrates, natural sugars & vitamins.
- Vegetables provide amino acids, minerals, salts, enzymes.
- Fresh fruits are cleansers of the body.
- Fresh vegetables are regenerators and builders.
- Live enzymes help to replenish new cellular growth

In-Depth Juicing

Quoted and referenced from several reputable sources as an education and testament to the benefits of eating a live food diet.

"Degeneration is the gradual deterioration of specific tissues, cells, or organs with corresponding impairment or loss of function, caused by injury, disease, or aging. Most professionals agree that degenerative diseases are preventable. Many believe some of the degenerative conditions are reversible if severe damage has not been done.

There are many factors that contribute to degeneration such as: improper diet and nutrition, inadequate exercise, rest and water amounts and excessive toxins. The automobile is a perfect example to illustrate what happens when the wrong ingredients are added to a working machine. If one were to put sand in the gas tank and sugar in the engine, the automobile would be ruined in a very short time. Our bodies work in the same manner however fortunately our bodies are a little more forgiving. Many people misuse the fact that our bodies are so forgiving. Degenerative diseases are earned from a lifetime of abuse.

In order for the body to use food given to it, it must first be broken down. Digestion disengages vitamins, minerals and other nutrients within food while breaking down carbohydrates, fats and proteins to smaller, utilizable molecules. Carbohydrates and fats are fuel sources. Proteins can be used for fuel but are usually used for reconstruction within the body. Enzymes are responsible for breaking down food. If food is not in its most basic form (amino acids, monosaccharide, small polysaccharides, fatty acids) when it enters the bloodstream, the body will identify these large molecules as foreign bodies; thus causing an immune response. Incomplete digestion also prevents vitamins, minerals and other nutrients from being separated from the food therefore rendered useless. Ironically enough enzymes require vitamins, mineral and nutrients in order to function. Gas, bloating, indigestion, heart burn and other digestion discomforts can be due to improper breakdown of food.

Enzymes come from live foods and are easily destroyed. Enzymes help in the absorption and break down of foods and supplements that we consume each day. When the body is not well and/or has imbalances, then it is common to find that natural enzyme levels have been depleted. This is why it is important to not only eat foods with many live enzymes, but to supplement with enzymes to help to absorption and digestion process. Heat, storage, pesticides, chemicals and genetic engineering all leave enzymes worthless. Your body has the ability to produce enzymes, but enzyme production will not be at optimal levels when the body is unwell.

Over-taxation of the digestive system as a whole can lead to many degenerative diseases. The average American diet is demanding of the digestive system. This is due to most of it being cooked and consisting of material that is difficult for the body to digest (grains, saturated or hydrogenated fats, large sugar molecules, dairy, etc)."

Juicing is the perfect tool to restore health and prevent disease.

"During the time of restoring health and for preventative measures, it makes sense to rest the digestive system. The fiber is separated from the nutrients and water when a fruit or vegetable is juiced allowing the body to receive the healing properties of food in a short amount of time because it can enter the bloodstream directly while resting the digestive system. Resting the digestive system gives the body an opportunity to focus its energy toward healing the body."

"The nutrition juice provides to the body is invaluable. Enzymes are in fresh, raw fruit and vegetable juices as well as vitamins, minerals and other nutrients. Other properties and nutrients of juice are being continually found. It is suspected that researchers will continue to find attributes concerning whole foods and probably never find others. Because nutrients are added to multi-vitamins/multi-minerals only after they are discovered, studied and deemed useful, it is quite possible there are nutrients unique to untreated, wholesome vegetable and fruit juice. Another redeeming quality of juice is the composition and arrangement of nutrients which allow the body to maximize absorption and utilization of them."

"Canned, bottled and frozen juices do not have the nutrient and therapeutic value that fresh juices have. Not only do most of them contain too much sugar, but the process they have gone through to become bottled, canned or frozen has stripped them of their natural vitamins, minerals, enzymes and other nutrients by way of heating, storage, being treated with chemicals, etc."

"Organic, un-waxed, fresh, raw fruits and vegetables are most ideal to use for juicing. If these are not available, below are some methods to wash produce. This method is the simplest we've found: Fill your sink with cold water; add a few tablespoons of salt and the juice of half a lemon. Soak the produce for approximately ten minutes, then rinse. There is also the possibility of buying a natural, commercial produce cleanser. For fruits that are commonly waxed, such as apples, it is recommended that you dip the fruit into boiling water for five seconds and then lift it out of the water with tongs."

Different juices yield different results. The basic varieties are as follows:

"**Fruit** — Fruit juices are generally thought of as cleansing, refreshing and they offer a quick burst of energy. The high water content flushes the digestive tract and kidneys, as well as purifies the bloodstream. Grapes, apples and lemons are all strong purifiers. Fruit juices are high in sugars; although these sugars are natural, the amount you drink should be modified (especially those who have been advised to limit sugar consumption)."

"**Carrot and Carrot Combinations** — Carrot juice is generally thought of as being an energy drink. Carrot juice is sweet, so it's often recommended to mix carrots with other vegetables to cut back on sweets. When you're making carrot combination juices, the carrot proportion should always dominate. Unless they are organic, carrots should be trimmed about ½ inch from the green because that's where pesticides are concentrated. Organic carrots do not need to be trimmed, just washed."

"**Green Juices** — This is what is thought of as "serious" juice. Green juices are healing, stabilizing and calming; the energy they offer is centering. They are best enjoyed in the evening. Green juices are a potent cocktail of nutrition. Because green juices are so powerful, unless they are diluted with some carrot or apple juice, they can cause lightheadedness and gastric distress. Only about a quarter of your glass should be green juice, with the rest being carrot, apple, or a combination of the two. Vegetables that can be used for green juices are alfalfa sprouts, barley greens, cabbage, kale, dandelion greens, green chard, lettuce varieties, parsley, spinach, and wheat grass."

"**The Unjuicables** — These fruits and vegetables yield so little water, at best they can leave you with very little to drink and at worst they can damage your juicer. When you see commercial juices with any of the below ingredients, it is usually the pulp of the fruit mixed with a lot of apple or grape juice."

• Apricots	• Cantaloupes	• Peaches
• Avocados	• Coconuts	• Plums/Prunes
• Bananas	• Honeydew Melons	• Strawberries
• Blueberries	• Papayas	

"It is best to wash and chop your produce right before juicing, and to drink it right after juicing, otherwise your juice rapidly loses nutritional potency. While it is best to drink juices right after they are made, they should be slowly sipped rather than gulped. Oranges, tangerines and grapefruit should be peeled before juicing, but use a vegetable peeler so as to just remove the rind, not the nutrient rich, white pith. The reason these particular fruits should be peeled is because their skins contain toxic substances and are also somewhat bitter. Also, apple seeds contain some cyanide so it is recommended that they be removed."

"When you're making a vegetable juice that contains produce that has a stronger odor, like garlic and ginger, the stronger smelling items should be among the first to be juiced so the ones that follow can push the last remnants through. Because of digestion considerations, fruits and vegetables generally should not mix together, with the exception of apples and carrots. Like herbs, juices are specific to the organs they strengthen and conditions they are used for."

Below is a list from a book written by Elson M. Hass, M.D. – *"Staying Healthy with Nutrition."*

Fruit Juices

Lemons — Liver, gallbladder, allergies, asthma, cardiovascular disease (CVD), colds

Citrus — CVD, obesity, hemorrhoids, varicose veins

Apple – liver, intestines

Pear – gallbladder

Grape – colon, anemia

Papaya – stomach, indigestion, hemorrhoids, colitis

Pineapple – allergies, arthritis, inflammation, edema, hemorrhoids

Watermelon – kidneys, edema

Black Cherry – colon, menstrual problems, gout

Vegetable Juices

Greens – CVD, skin, eczema, digestive problems, obesity

Spinach – anemia, eczema

Parsley – kidneys, edema, arthritis

Beet Greens – gallbladder, liver, osteoporosis

Watercress – anemia, colds

Wheatgrass – anemia, liver intestines, breath

Cabbage – colitis, ulcer

Comfrey – intestines, hypertension, osteoporosis

Carrots – eyes, arthritis, osteoporosis

Beets – blood, liver, menstrual problems, arthritis

Celery – kidneys, diabetes, osteoporosis

Cucumber – edema, diabetes

Jerusalem Artichokes – diabetes

Garlic – allergies, colds, hypertension, CVD, diabetes

Radish – liver, obesity

Potatoes – intestines, ulcer

*Buy a good juice book and salad book to give variety to this program. It is essential to rotate fruits and vegetable when doing this program to provide balance and a full spectrum of nutrients.

chapter four:
Womb for Improvement

There are many among us that would do practically anything to be their child's advocate, if only they could have children. When I am educating couples about healthy children, it starts right in the womb. Would you want to buy or live in a home if you knew that your contractor had only poured half of the foundation on which your home was built? How about if he didn't shingle your roof and also put in plumbing that would leak, flood and damage your house? What if he mostly did a good job, except he cut a few corners here and there, like faulty electrical work? Maybe the quality of your house is pretty good, but the city happened to give you a building permit on an old sewage dumping site. God is your architect. You are the contractor. Would you give your child a body with a faulty foundation, faulty wiring of the nervous system, a weak lymphatic and digestive system if you could prevent it? Would you dare get pregnant with a body that you had treated like a dump site? People are doing it every day. You can do better!

However, sometimes we can do everything right, doing our very best, and something still doesn't work out the way that we think that it should. When our child has challenges, we can not waste time feeling guilty or playing the blame game. We have to get to work being our child's advocate! I spoke already about knowing the guilt of having a sick child, and that I unknowingly contributed to our rough start. I also knew that nobody would love my children, protect and help them more than I could. Guilt is an excuse to do nothing, to be immobile, instead of an immoveable force in advocating the best life possible for your child.

Did you notice that when I started this chapter I referred to educating couples? Unless something dramatic has changed recently, and women don't need sperm to get pregnant anymore, I am talking to the two equally contributing entities making up the embryo. Yes, you men are contributing half of the life force to this child and should be equally enthusiastic about getting yourself as healthy as possible before you make your initial contribution.

There has been a growing amount of information on prenatal care, but what about pre-prenatal care, getting healthy before you conceive. Both men and women are responsible to get their bodies into a healthy state before the egg and sperm are introduced. Couples should consider nutrition, supplements, detoxification and natural hormone balancing together, not just for the woman because she happens to be the one carrying the child in her womb.

Especially for Men

There are a variety of factors that can negatively impact sperm health and therefore have an impact on chances of getting pregnant, or contributing healthy sperm including but not limited to:

- Tight clothing, including underwear
- Too many hot baths
- Smoking
- Inactivity
- Vitamin/mineral deficiency
- Malnutrition
- Immune system disorders
- Candida
- Drugs: recreational or prescribed
- Excessive alcohol use
- Caffeine consumptions
- Coffee
- Recent or reoccurring infections or illnesses, including a cold or the flu
- Previous infections or illnesses, and/or their treatment, including mumps, chlamydia and radiotherapy treatment
- Stress, especially untreated chronic stress
- Work hazards, including exposure to heavy metals, solvents and x-rays
- Environmental toxins
- Hormonal imbalances

Studies done recently show that consumption of even moderate amounts of coffee, around 3 cups a day, can affect a man's ability to have normal and/or healthy children. Several studies have been conducted to show the adverse effect of modern life on the quality and quantity of sperm. One report on the research by scientist at Bradford University and the University of California, Berkeley, done on normal men between 22 to 80, was published in the journal Human Reproduction and concluded: "Independent of age, men with substantial daily caffeine consumption have increased sperm DNA damage."

The damage to the DNA has been linked to genetic defect, cancer and infertility in the children of these men. Dr. Andrew Wyrobek, the lead author, stated that the damage was of the type which leads to chromosomal rearrangement in the embryo, which can lead to death of the fetus, birth defects, cancer or genetic disease in the babies which are born.

It is not certain how the DNA damage happens, but it is happening. Many scientists collectively have the opinion that our current lifestyle, combined with stress and environmental pollutants has affected the quantity, and I might add, the quality of the sperm produced. Research has shown that younger men are not as fertile as their fathers. Back to that pre-World War II diet!

Other factors that contribute to low or damaged sperm are:
- Taking anti-depressants
- Over usage of mobile phones
- Sitting for long hours at a desk job
- Immobility for long periods of time, for example: truck drivers
- Sitting with a laptop on the lap
- Pre-prenatal and prenatal health

Does What I Eat Matter?

Yes, yes, yes! A diet high in plant sterols, which are easily converted to human estrogen and progesterone in the body, has been shown to reduce or eliminate menopausal symptoms and support the body's efforts in hormone balance, including conception. Plant sterols are hormone precursors, not chemically synthetic hormones, so your body can take and make whatever it needs.

What precursor foods will readily convert into estrogen and progesterone to assist the body in hormone balance and regulation?

• Soy	• Raw Nuts	• Garlic
• Flax Seed	• Seeds	• Wheat Germ
• Yams	• Papaya	• Avocados
• Peas	• Bananas	• Leafy Greens
• Cucumbers	• Licorice Root	
• Bee Pollen	• Raw Fruits and Vegetables	

*Note many of these foods are live foods, which were discussed in chapter three.

Which supplements are precursors to the body to support natural hormone production?

- Evening Primrose Oil
- Flax Seed Oil
- Wild Yam

The goal is to help the body help itself by providing the most natural healing environment we can. When introducing foods that are estrogen and progesterone precursors, the body doesn't replace lost hormones with synthetics but instead stimulates the body to correct its own hormone imbalances. Symptoms result not from a shortage, but from the body trying to get back into balance. The body is amazing and somewhat forgiving. When we correct are errors and shift our paradigm of thinking, and allow our body to regenerate and heal, it will usually step up and do the job that it was designed to do. It may not happen overnight, in one week, one month, one year, but it will make every effort. Ask yourself, "How long did it take me or my child to earn our current health?" Answer that question and then be reasonable about your healing time. The body heals in a much more quickly compared to the time it took in breaking it down, but it needs patience and persistence to heal.

Creating and maintaining hormone balance requires:

- Consuming caffeine and alcohol in extreme moderation
- Practicing stress management techniques
- Taking supplementation to rebuild immune system
- Eating a natural precursor diet
- Using natural hormone replacement
- Eliminating harmful substances and foods from your lifestyle
- Regular exercise
- Proper hydration/water consumption
- You must recognize that you are always in control

Symptoms are always a late manifestation of a breakdown in the body. We know that as the body goes through the progression of disease and our immune system breaks down, hormonal imbalance almost always comes into play. The breakdown generally occurs long before the symptoms surface. When symptoms surface it is an immediate call to action.

Act quickly and get back on track. Better yet, keep your body healthy so that symptoms do not need to act as a warning signal to you that a break down is on its way.

Start early thinking about contributing healthy eggs or sperm to your unborn child. Act responsibly and quickly to keep you and your unborn child healthy when you find out you are indeed pregnant. Smile and be joyful that you are making conscious efforts to improve one day at a time.

Hormones in Women

Any one particular hormonal imbalance in the body slightly throws off all hormones. Our immune system and our hormonal system have a direct impact on one another. When our immune system has been compromised, hormonal imbalance almost always come into play.

If there is too much estrogen (synthetic or natural) in the body, it can lead to risks of: invasive breast cancer, heart attacks, blood clots, osteoporosis, dementia, strokes, and less minor conditions such as weight gain, mood swings, salt and fluid retention, migraine headaches, heavy blood flow, depression, anxiety and insomnia.

When we have unopposed estrogen, the bodies inability to recognize or balance an excess or deficiency, this can lead to hot flashes and night sweats. I would recommend using a progesterone precursor, such Wild Yam Cream, to regulate unopposed symptoms. By using precursors to stimulate the body's ability to produce progesterone, the balancing hormone in the body, it allows the body to recognize and balance most hormone ailments.

When you are young your body needs more estrogen. The reason for this is that your estrogen needs increase dramatically during prime child bearing years. Unfortunately, due to poor dietary habits, lack of exercise and water intake, sleep habits and stress we have a hard time keeping up with the demands of our hormonal system. This can cause an estrogen shortage in the body that leads to menstrual cramps, bloated and puffiness, heavy blood flow, mood swing, fatigue, and many other PMS symptoms. I recommend using use balancing herbs to help our body make all of the necessary hormones, mostly estrogen, needed during this time when we want to conceive.

Good balancing herbs consist of: Blessed Thistle, Damiana, Kava Kava, Serenoa Serrulata, Dong Quai, Raspberry Leaf, Passion Flower, Licorice Root, Black Cohosh, Passion Flower, Cramp Bark, Parsley, and Motherwort. Different combinations of these herbs have been shown to help the body in a precursor capacity for estrogen, cortisol and testosterone balancing. They are all readily available at your local health food store and from many health professionals. If you are interested in a formula that combines all of these herbs in a natural, filler-free formula, the M'lis Company sells Balance. I have personally used it myself and with clients, with fantastic results.

As we age our bodies finally catch up with the demands for estrogen. When we are past those childbearing years we do not need the abundant supply of estrogen anymore. Again, due to poor diet, lack of exercise and water intake, stress and lack of sleep, we do not have enough progesterone available in our body to balance the estrogen levels, and we end up with too much estrogen. This can lead to: depression, anxiety, rapid weight gain, salt and fluid retention, foggy thought process, and many other menopausal symptoms. Use Wild Yam Cream to help your body produce and regulate progesterone levels. This helps with the regulation of all hormones in creating a balanced hormonal environment in the body.

Any natural hormone program will take at least 90 days to start effectively regulating and balancing the body's hormonal system. Remember, we are helping the body help itself, not drugging it with chemicals. In order to put your body in a healing environment, you need to have a diet that consists mostly of raw healthy foods, drink at least half of your body weight in ounces, exercise regularly, use stress management techniques and get enough sleep. Most individuals will need to repeat this at least once a year to keep their hormones balanced.

Get healthy before conception and then do everything you can to stay healthy during your pregnancy.

Questions to Ask Yourself During Pregnancy

YES NO
- ❏ ❏ Do you rest when you feel weary?
- ❏ ❏ Are you getting enough sleep at night?
- ❏ ❏ Do you eat regularly?
- ❏ ❏ Do you eat healthy well balanced meals, or high fat, high sugar or fast foods?
- ❏ ❏ Are you staying hydrated?
- ❏ ❏ Are you exercising and staying fit throughout your pregnancy?
- ❏ ❏ Do you take health supplements every day recommended by your health care provider?
- ❏ ❏ Do you have prenatal check up regularly?
- ❏ ❏ Have you prepared, or are you preparing financially and emotionally for the amazing changes that parenthood will bring.

Tips for Sleeping Success

A study by researchers at the UCSF School of Nursing has concluded that women, who have less sleep or severely disrupted sleep in late pregnancy, show a highly increased risk of having longer labors and are much more likely to have cesarean births.

The study found that women who averaged less than six hours of sleep per night had significantly longer labors and were 4.5 times more likely to have cesarean deliveries than women who averaged seven or more hours of sleep. Even more profound, women who averaged between six and seven hours of sleep per night were 3.7 times more likely to have a cesarean delivery. The study appears in the December 2008 issue of the American Journal of Obstetrics and Gynecology.

The study assessed the sleeping patterns and habits of 131 women in their ninth month of pregnancy. Study findings reveled that women, who were sleeping less than six hours per night, had an average labor of 29 hours. In comparison, women who slept seven or more hours per night had an average labor of 17.7 hours. Call me easy to please, but shaving more than 10 hours off of my labor time is awfully appealing, instead of just awful!

Sometimes we can feel desperate for a good night's sleep. However appealing getting that sleep may be, remember that over-the-counter sleep aids, including herbal remedies, are not recommended for pregnant women.

Following the next few examples provided by KidsHealth for Parents, may safely improve your chances of getting a good night's sleep:

- Cut out caffeinated drinks like soda, coffee, and tea from your diet as much as possible. Restrict any intake of them to the morning or early afternoon.

- Avoid drinking a lot of fluids or eating a full meal within a few hours of going to bed at night. (But make sure that you also get plenty of nutrients and liquids throughout the day.) Some women find it helpful to eat more at breakfast and lunch and then have a smaller dinner. If nausea is keeping you up, you may want to eat a few crackers before you go to bed.

- Get into a routine of going to bed and waking up at the same time each day.

- Avoid rigorous exercise right before you go to bed. Instead, do something relaxing, like soaking in a warm bath for 15 minutes or having a warm, caffeine-free drink, such as milk with honey or a cup of herbal tea.

- If a leg cramp awakens you, it may help to press your feet hard against the wall or to stand on the leg. Also, make sure that you're getting enough calcium in your diet, which can help reduce leg cramps.

- Take a class in yoga or learn other relaxation techniques to help you unwind after a busy day. (Be sure to discuss any new activity or fitness regimen with your doctor first.)

- If fear and anxiety are keeping you awake, consider enrolling in a child birth or parenting class. More knowledge and the company of other pregnant women may help to ease the fears that are keeping you awake at night.

Induced Labor

The birth of my son was an induced labor, which I requested, because my doctor, whom I respected, trusted and adored, was leaving the country over my due date. I was afraid that I would go into labor while he was away, and may have to undergo another C-Section, as with my first baby. It all sounded pretty tidy and easy to have scheduled birth. Knowing what I know now, I would NEVER do this again. I felt in my mother's gut, that some of the challenges my son has faced was partly due to my choice for induced labor. I had an "Aha" moment doing research for this book. I felt that I should have made a different choice. Now I know why. After reading this study, what my gut knew coincided with the research, and the pieces of the puzzle finally fit for me. Here is one of the studies:

The Brave New World of Evidence-Based Maternity Care for 21st Century: Autism and Pitocin Induction

"In July 2000, a cover story for Newsweek was about an explosive increase in childhood autistic disorders, a severe problem in which the majority of these children wind up institutionalized by the age of 13. One of the possible explanations mentioned was a statistical link between the increase in autism and the increase in labors induced with Pitocin. It quoted Dr. Eric Hollander (director of an autism clinic at Mt Sinai Medical Center in New York) as reporting that 60% of his patients were the product of a Pitocin-induced labor. The article identified that more children suffer from the scourge of autism than childhood cancer or Downs Syndrome, as high as 1 out of 500."

I can only imagine what kind of nightmare it would be for the maker of this drug, if that observation turns out to have merit. Many nurses jokingly refer to this drug as "Vitamin P."

"In the last few years, public health authorities have identified an enormous increase in the incidence of childhood autism. In California, the number of kids receiving state services for autistic disorders has nearly quadrupled since 1987. (6) A recent news report on National Public Radio noted 775 news cases, a 33% increase over the previous quarter in which only 550 new cases were identified. This brain development disorder results in a lack of normal language skills and inability to form human bonds of affection with parents and other people. The majority of its victims are boys. Many also suffer from epilepsy. The physical, mental, emotional and social disabilities combined are so sever that most autistic children end up in institutions by the age of 13. This is a tragedy for the child and its parents, a loss to society and an economic burden of great proportion. Autism is now thought to affect one person in 500, making it more common than Down's syndrome or childhood cancer. According to Dr Marie Bristol Power from the National Institute of Child Health and Human Development, it is a not a rare disorder but a 'pressing public-health problem'."

"Neither the cause of this disorder nor the reason for its exponential increase is well understood by researchers at this time. However there is data associating autistic disorders with the use of an artificial hormone (Pitocin) which is given to pregnant women to induce or speed up labor (6,7). Pitocin is a synthetic exogenous source of the natural hormone oxytocin which stimulates the gravid uterus to contract. It was developed as a drug by the Parke-Davis pharmaceutical company in 1953 and put into general use in 1955. It comes from the pituitary glands of cattle and includes acetic acid for pH adjustment and .5 percent chloretone as a preservative. The lead story in the July 31, 2000 issue Newsweek magazine was devoted to exploring this growing health problem. Material published by the World Health Organization also notes an association between the use of Pitocin and autistic disorders."

"In spontaneous labors the mother's pituitary gland makes an endogenous (i.e. internal) oxytocin that triggers the physiological onset and progress of labor. The hormone oxytocin is also produced during breastfeeding (causing the let-down of breast milk) and it accompanies sexual orgasm. For this reason it is referred to as the "love hormone" by obstetrician Christian Northrop, MD as each of these biological events are associated with experiences of great emotional bonding and include meaningful social interaction between the individuals involved. Since autistic disorders produce an inability to make or maintain affectionate bonds or have normal social relationships, one cannot help but wonder if perhaps there is a causal relationship between these disorders and exogenous sources of an artificial form of oxytocin. Perhaps flooding the immature body of the fetus (especially boy babies) with this gender-specific synthetic hormone from animals somehow interferes with the eventual function of these psychological systems. It is an intriguing question."

"However, Pitocin is not the only drug received by women whose labors are being induced or augmented. The use of Pitocin requires that the mother also be given IV fluids, have continuous electric fetal monitoring in place and remain sedentary in her hospital bed while connected to this equipment. Pitocin-induced uterine contractions and enforced maternal immobility makes labor more painful, so much so that under these circumstances most laboring women also receive narcotic pain relievers and/or epidural anesthesia. The use of these drugs and anesthetics is also associated with an increase in operative deliveries (vacuum extraction or forceps). It is possible that the causative agent or trigger event for autism is a particular combination of drugs or certain physical problems or propensity for either the mother or baby, in combination with certain drugs, rather than a simple direct effect of Pitocin per se."

"The use of Pitocin to induce or augment labors and concomitant use of epidural anesthesia has been steadily climbing for the last 20 years – about the same period that the increase in autism has been reported. Estimates of the use of Pitocin in laboring women over the last 2 decades range from 12% to 60%. However, a 1992 survey by a medical anthropologist at the University of Texas found that 81% of women in US hospital receive Pitocin to either induce or augment labor. Epidural use is as high as 95% in many urban hospitals. When one factors in a Cesarean rate of 23% (acknowledging some overlap), the proportions of these facts is staggering as virtually 100% of medically-managed births are subjected to a high level of pharmaceutical interventions that have never been approved for use in fetuses. It certainly seems prudent to research the possible association with pharmaceutically-augmented labors in an attempt to discover the cause of the rising tide of autistic disorders. It may be necessary to amend our current obstetrical practices to prevent an epidemic of this expensive and emotionally-crippling disorder."

It should also be noted that there is a lot of up and coming research linking the contribution of these drugs and medications to the rise ADD/ADHD. Diet and lifestyle choices could have an impact on whether or not these conditions are exacerbated or even triggered in the system at all. I would like to restate that knowing what I know now, I would NOT make the choice to induce labor for the sake of convenience.

Exceptions:

When the mother or the fetus is in danger or distress, it may be medically necessary to induce labor, and the benefits of induction would far outweigh any potential risks. I WOULD choose induction in this case, as the life of my child and my own life is a valuable gift from God. I do not believe that induction should be considered lightly or for the convenience of yourself, your doctor, so that you can have your baby on a specific date, or because you are tired of being pregnant. I believe the desire for instant gratification, the desire to not be inconvenienced or uncomfortable, and just the plain desire to have control over all things has led us down the path of abuse in many areas of our lives, including induction of labor. I am thankful for the medical knowledge and choices that we have in this day and age and to have these medical capabilities which can save lives. I am also grateful for the ability to study and gain my own knowledge so that I can make more educated decisions on what is best for me and my children. You have the same power.

chapter five:
Rights and Insights

God gave us parental inspiration to direct and guide our children. So why do we sometimes ignore it? Are we afraid that we might be judged harshly by our family, friends, neighbors, children's teachers or medical professionals? Probably. We have all felt this way at one time or another. The difference between somebody who is their child's advocate, and somebody who is not, is that the advocate may have thoughts or feelings of fear, helplessness or inadequacy, but forges down the path anyway. Nothing will stop the advocate from doing what is best for their child even when gut instinct is all they have in the beginning. We must be an advocate for our children's health and wellbeing. We can not solely leave the critical decisions about their health up to others, including doctors.

We have a right to ask questions until we are satisfied with the answer given.

We have the right to as many opinions as we think we may need in order to give our children the best care available.

We have a right to say no to medication that we feel may be harmful to our child.

We have a right to disagree with suggestions or opinions about our child's care if we feel that they are being compromised or will have unacceptable side effects.

We have a right to access and implement allopathic medicine and naturopathic medicine, or a combination of both for our children.

We have a right not to feel guilty when we don't conform to what society or the medical community thinks we should do for or with our children.

We have the right to be good parents when we take responsibility for our own actions and protect our children by doing a lot of research and asking many questions.

We have the right to love our children unconditionally.

Inspiration comes in many forms. I have realized over the years that we are here in this life to serve, help and inspire one another. Many times my inspiration for helping my children has come from talking with others and most importantly, listening to what is being said. We must be teachable, not just open minded, but really teachable. That does not mean that we do everything that anyone tells us to do. It means that we research, talk, and listen. Then we carefully weigh and consider the information we have been given in combination with our child's personality, strengths, weaknesses, and our available resources to make the most of our children's opportunities. Then, and only then, can we implement changes to help our children and ourselves.

Being teachable can be very painful. It requires us to self examine and recognize our weaknesses and challenges. Being teachable also requires us to be willing to do the work necessary to bring about change so that we can help ourselves and our families. We must help our children be teachable by our example. We must be willing to adapt to change and listen to what our children are telling us, through their speech, actions, emotions, and nonverbal communication.

Your life is like a beautiful garden that God has planted. He wants you fertilize your garden of life each day with uplifting things that strengthen the fruits of your labors so that you and your family can have joy. We are not teachable when we are in denial or are unwilling to put forth the effort to "weed our gardens."

Good Fertilizer

Drink plenty of water, about half your body weight in ounces each day. (example: Weight 100 lbs., drink at least 50 oz. of water each day)

Manage stress.

Get plenty of sleep each night.

Get live food at every meal and strive towards making more of your diet live foods.

Eat whole grains, as they are the staff of life.

Eat lean proteins to build and maintain strength, but do not overindulge.

Use healthy oils sparingly, cold-pressed oils like Olive, Sunflower, and Safflower Oils.

Exercise regularly 30 min. each day.

Practice with your children the principals of gratitude.

Look for service opportunities for your family.

Be in the moment with your family, pay attention to what is happening right now!

Take daily supplements to supply nutrients that may be lacking in your family's diet.

Spend time laughing every day with your children, and try to laugh when you feel frustrated.

Get organized and help your children stay organized, everyone feels better when things go smoothly.

God also wants you to weed your garden of life so that the fruits of your labors are not entangled with poisonous or innocuous plants that will take root and suffocate the healthy thriving plants that you want to bloom and desire to harvest.

Bad Weeds

Eliminate refined sugar from your family's diet. Sugar causes inflammation and suppresses the immune system. When your family is sick, you cannot "treat" yourself. When you are well, you should only have refined sugar occasionally, in moderation.

Eliminate red meat and pork from your family's diet. These meats should only be eaten, if at all, in moderation. The consistency of these meats and the toxin content, contribute to a very slow digestion time in your body. I recommend not having putrefied waste sitting in your system on a regular basis, which is what you have if you consume large amounts of meat, especially red meat. Stinky….Pee Yew! Eat fresh fish several times a week and small amounts of poultry instead.

No caffeine, which is found in coffee, soda, and some medication. The diuretic properties of caffeine robe the body of potassium, important minerals and cleansing fluids. Often, we drink less water because we do not feel thirsty after drinking a soda or coffee, which further dehydrates our bodies, acting as a diuretic and robbing our bodies of necessary liquids.

Do not cook with or consume hydrogenated oils.

Cut down on television time. Television viewing in childhood and adolescence is associated with health problems and conditions in adulthood such as: overweight or obesity, poor fitness, smoking, and raised cholesterol levels. Excessive viewing could possibly have long-lasting adverse effects on health.

Pay attention to what your children are watching. Turn off the television if you see or hear inappropriate material coming into your home. Would you allow those "people" on television to do what they are doing or say what they are saying, if they were doing it right in your living room? They are, if you allow that programming in your home. Television can be a negative stimulus in your home. Watch your children's behavior after being under the influence of certain television shows. It's eye opening to see the influence programs can have on our kids, some subtle, some not so subtle. Is this program benefiting your child in a positive way, or at least not harming them with examples of negative or disrespectful behavior? I found that the cartoon violence and mouthy disrespectful cartoon characters, and other live actor's portrayal of behaviors, on kid's shows, was contributing to some of the negative behavior in my home. When I became much more conscientious of what my kids were watching, not using the TV as a babysitter, I started limiting total TV time and show content. Our home has become more peaceful.

Over stimulus of electronic devices can have a negative impact on our children. It has been estimated that over 10.5 Billion US Dollars was spent world wide on electronic games for use in the home in 1993. This raises the question as to why more research has not been undertaken to determine if the high use of the games will affect the users. I guess the huge profits from the sale of the games are discouraging any research studies that may prove the games are potentially detrimental to the users. I believe that the prolonged and excessive use of electronic games contribute to obsessive, addictive behavior, desensitizing of feelings, health problems and possible development of anti-social behavior as well as other disorders. I do not believe that electronic devices are inherently evil. My family and I enjoy modern technology in full spectrum. However, I believe these devices should be used with adult supervision, discretion, and in moderation. We have truly lost meaning of moderation in all things. Just THINK, that's all I am asking. Don't just mindlessly let outside influences in your home where they can bombard your children.

Limit dairy intake to the least evasive dairy products like cream cheese, cottage cheese, ricotta cheese, plain yogurt and small amounts of real butter. Dairy consumption of milk, ice cream, sour cream and hard cheese can cause digestive problems, mucus in the body and allergies. If you or your child is experiencing digestive programs or allergies, milk and other dairy products is one of the things I would cut from the family diet. Remember, we are not cows! We don't want to look like cows! We are the only mammal that continues to drink milk once weaned from our mother. Interesting food for thought.

chapter six:
The Myth of Instant Gratification

I feel that more and more we are giving up what we want most for what we want at the moment. We constantly have messages drilled into our heads that we should be able to have anything that we want, whenever we want it. This message has also helped to breed selfishness, laziness and a sense of entitlement. The state of our general economy, increasing crime rate, overwhelming debt and rising number of over weight and obese individuals in our nation are a few results of The Myth of Instant Gratification, which states, "Treat yourself, you deserve it, and deal with the consequences later." Later is here! You can't afford to buy into this Myth, especially when your family's entire well being rests in keeping our families strong in mind, body and spirit.

We want to do all things the easy way, painless way, and we want to make sure that it is almost effortless. In the day and age of modern technology, we often get this wish. It is no wonder why our children are growing up with ideas of entitlement due to the mere fact that they were born. We have a whole generation of kids wanting to start at the top and work their way sideways through life. It is not possible for most of us to have and maintain good health with little or no effort. It is a conscious daily task to combat cravings, overcome media hype, dodge pharmaceutical pitfalls, relearn how to shop, read labels, and motivate ourselves to exercise. This is a real war, a war that our families are currently losing. It's plain old fashioned hard work! We must practice conscious living in which we keep ourselves in the present and aware of the moment to moment choices we make all day long. It eventually becomes second nature and the rewards far outweigh the feelings of boot camp!

Every day I still think, really think, about what I am eating, especially when "treating" myself. I ask myself why I am eating what I am eating. Children are not too young to be taught a simple version of this concept. When you prepare healthy food, briefly talk to your family about what great benefits these foods have for the body. Make it fun! Have some friendly competition going on among family members for naming benefits or negatives about food that you are eating. Don't be too serious, but make learning fun! Give out little non-food prizes for the best answers at dinner or breakfast time.

The ultimate teaching experiences begin early. Start when your children are small so that they learn to love healthy food and begin to understand the benefits of eating well early on. It is so much easier to stay healthy than to back track through unhealthy habits and bad health. Remember, if your family has gotten off track, you can take control and get healthy again.

You must want to get healthy.

You must know how to get healthy.

You must have every opportunity to do what it takes to get healthy.

Individuals and/or parents are in charge of wanting to get healthy, it's a personal choice. This book provides information on how to get healthier. Each person is in charge of creating the opportunities for their family to get healthy and stay well. We must seek opportunity by opening our eyes to possibilities. Again, it comes back to being teachable.

I teach a course for health spas and clinics that has to do with attitude. I have been helping to inspire individuals to choose better health for themselves and their families for years. When I first became well, I wanted to shout to the whole world, "You don't have to be unhealthy and sick! You can be well like me!" I was shocked when I didn't get the response of overwhelming gratitude and interest from people. I thought everybody that was sick, especially with the same disorders I had previously had, would be begging me to share how I got well. Why didn't everyone want to be well like me? I began to realize that not everyone was teachable or ready to learn what I wanted to share. I can place most individuals into three categories of readiness. Which one are you?

The Sufferer

This is the person who is getting something out of being sick. Their illness has often become their identity. They often enjoy poor health on some level. They are heard regularly complaining and talking about their ailments to anyone who will listen to them. These individuals may tell you that they want to get well and even attempt "new" medications or health regiments, but they don't really want to let go of the illness. They don't usually follow through with anything that might make them well. The pay off for staying sick is far too rewarding to get well. Comfort can often be found in the familiar, even if that is illness. People often expect less of us because we are "sick." If you are this person, only you can let go and become teachable. You must stop hiding behind this unhealthy mask. You must want to enjoy good health and all the blessings that it will bring into your life. People who enjoy bad health create tremendous burdens, not only for themselves, but for everyone around them.

The Arguer

This person wants to argue about how they are "special" and nobody has solutions that can help them. They, like the sufferer, have often tried EVERYTHING. Perhaps, they have tried many things that have not worked, but I doubt with the right attitude and mind set. Besides, you should NEVER give up! This person likes to make excuses about why it won't work for them. They have done it all and already have all the answers. Again, these individuals are not teachable. It you are this person and you want to change, you must be willing to listen, consider, and implement different choices into your life after weighing all your options. I don't waste my breath arguing with anybody. You wouldn't have asked my opinion or read this book IF you had all the answers. So my reply is this, "If what you are doing is working, you should probably keep doing it." If you are sick or unhealthy, what you're doing isn't working! Arguing and negativity feeds bad health and keeps you sick. You can't keep doing the same unhealthy things and expect good health to arrive miraculously one day.

The Doer

This person, although maybe fearful of failure, is willing to do whatever it takes to recapture health and achieve wellness. This person is teachable. These are the only people I work with. They do not follow along blindly like sheep, but ask questions and open their mind to learning about their bodies, environment and new choices. They are willing to try new things and work hard to regain their health. It is important to remember that outside of genetic conditions, we have earned our health. We contribute every day by what we do and don't do. These individuals understand that the journey is life long and that correcting bad health habits will not happen overnight. Our bodies are resilient and will respond quickly when placed in a good healthy environment, but it takes time. The Doer is committed and consistent. They also recognize that there is hope and that they have choices regarding their situation. Generally, this person has experienced what I call the "Aha" moment in their life regarding their health. I congratulate you if you are a Doer. Your life will be far more joyful and fulfilling than the Sufferer or the Arguer.

The "Aha Moment"

When the mind experiences distress, and we have tried many solutions that don't work, we become frustrated. I pray that this book helps you discover solutions for your family's health problems and creates of moment of discovery where you can say "Aha!" that is the answer I have been looking for. Perhaps I may help you find the missing piece to your family's health puzzle, or to look at things from a different perspective. These can be "Aha" moments.

Pure Belief is Powerful

I strongly caution against using the word curing. Healing and curing are different things. Sometimes it is not possible for us to cure ourselves, but it is still possible for us to help ourselves heal. The possibility of healing helps us to visualize and relate to illness and disability from a new and empowering perspective. We need to harness belief in our lives again, it is powerful and healing. At Christmas time I see trees and decorations with the word "Believe" displayed every where I look. I imagine that if we took that message to heart we could harness healing powers within ourselves that would eliminate much of the need for modern medicine. One of my favorite quotes is by Charles Swindoll and he says:

"The longer I live the more I realize the impact of attitude on life. Attitude, to me, is more important than facts. It is more important than the past, than education, than money, than circumstances, than failures, than successes, than what other people think or say or do. It is more important than appearance, giftedness or skill. It will make or break a company… a church… a home… a life. The remarkable thing is we have a choice every day regarding the attitude we will embrace for that day.

We cannot change the past — we cannot change the fact that people will act in a certain way. We cannot change the inevitable. The only thing we can do is play on the one string we have, and that is our attitude. I am convinced that life is 10% what happens to me and 90% how I react to it."

I believe that with the right attitude towards helping your family regain health, you have embraced the most important component achieving wellness. I believe in you!

Older children need to manage and take responsibility for their health. I have lost count of the number of parents that have decided to "make" their teens and adult children get healthy. You can not make an older child or adult child well by demanding it, buying them a wellness program, gym membership or supplements. They simply will not be well because you wish it. These are individuals with ideas, feelings, and choices, just like you.

When these children truly desire to change and get well, I have seen miraculous things happen. These younger bodies tend to bounce back and recover more quickly than older bodies as they have not experienced longer term damage and abuse that we subject ourselves to. The older children need to be taught to read labels, make their own healthy food choices, drink their water allotment, exercise and take supplements without our hovering over them every moment. If they want to be well, we need to teach them and then give them the opportunity to do what it takes to be successful.

I have had the experience of family members being dragged to my office to start a wellness program and it is usually ends poorly. The kids cheat on the program foods, refuse to exercise, and don't take their supplements. It is a battle of wills to see who will win. Let me tell you nobody wins. You will spend a lot of money and effort so that your child can waste valuable time and resources to show their independence and still remain sick and/or unhealthy.

I have also had the pleasure of working with children who want to be well. They work hard and stay the course, some days tearfully, but dutifully. These children have amazing success and acquire lifetime tools and habits to help them, not only stay healthy, but to accomplish other great challenges in their lives. My daughter, Hannah, asked me if I would reward her for going without sugar for one year. I told her that I would. This was more than a no soda challenge. It meant no refined sugar or artificial sweeteners. I gave her one free day on her birthday to "cheat". Occasionally, at different times throughout this year, she would ask me if she could have certain foods that she knew were not allowed on her "no sugar" program. My reply always stayed the same, "It's your choice." She chose not to indulge her whims and stayed the course. She completed the program for an entire year, because she wanted to succeed. It didn't hurt that I gave her $300 and some new clothes either. A little motivation can be encouraging, especially in tempting times.

chapter seven:
The Medication Craze

I am increasingly alarmed by the ever emerging theory of, "Just one pill and it's all down hill." This is a great lie that has been perpetrated to generations of the sick and the well seeking a quick fix to a health challenge. How many of us have wanted to just take a pill to make what ever ails us go away. I have. Maybe you have been sick, or your child's behavior or illness is making you "nuts." Maybe you and your family need to loose weight, balance your hormones, keep your hair from falling out, lower your cholesterol, blood pressure or treat anxiety or depression. There are pills for all of these things. It is quick and easy to swallow hope or desire in the form of a pill. No effort is needed or required in swallowing medication, but no quick fix will happen either. Do you seriously examine the medications that you are choosing to give your child?

YES NO
- ❏ ❏ Are you willing to deal with the side effects of the medication? Sometimes these side effects outweigh the benefits of taking the medication.
- ❏ ❏ Did you do your homework to see if there were any less evasive ways to treat your child's disorder, not easier, but less evasive, that would achieve long term healthy results?
- ❏ ❏ What other goals have you set to help your child correct the health challenge, besides taking medication?
- ❏ ❏ Is your doctor willing to help your child wean off of the medication as a change in health habits is made and the condition improves?
- ❏ ❏ Are giving your child medication just because it's easier than changing bad habits, behaviors or life style?

Ritalin the Big Lie

Would you knowingly give your child Meth? We hear about the increasing number of Meth addicts, but did you know that the name for Ritalin is Methylphenidate, notice the word Meth. Methylphenidate, or Ritalin, is a prescription stimulant commonly used to treat attention-deficit hyperactivity disorder, chronic fatigue disorder and narcolepsy, to name a few. In February 2005, a team of researchers from The University of Texas

M. D. Anderson Cancer Center led by R.A. El-Zein announced that a study of 12 children indicated that methylphenidate may be carcinogenic. In the study, 12 children were given standard therapeutic doses of methylphenidate. At the conclusion of the 3-month study, all 12 children displayed significant treatment-induced chromosomal aberrations."

It is widely accepted that methylphenidate is the closest pharmaceutical equivalent to cocaine. There are also studies that show that cocaine addicts cannot distinguish between the two drugs when both are intravenously administered. Cocaine, however, has a higher affinity for the dopamine receptor when compared to methylphenidate.

I remember, not so long ago, a fierce campaign of "Just Say No" to drugs, which has now turned to "Just Say Yes" to stimulants, narcotics, and a whole host of mind and mood altering drugs. I feel as though we are being tricked into thinking that there is a difference between what the pharmaceutical companies are pushing as "medically necessary" drugs and those "recreational" drugs that we know we shouldn't take. What's the difference anymore? The line isn't even gray, it's pretty black and white if you look at ingredients, side effects and long term potential for abuse, addiction and the permanent damage that many of the "medically necessary" drugs can cause. Do your homework, use your common sense and gut instincts. All medication isn't bad, but many can be deadly.

Medication itself is not the enemy. Our abuse of medication and desire for instant results and sense of powerlessness is the real enemy. We are our own worst enemy when we passively give medication to our children without researching and putting into place a long term plan for changes in life style. I am not opposed to medication usage. I have a deep respect for allopathic medicine and I am grateful for the choice to utilize modern medicine. I oppose blindly taking medication because we are told that it is the "only" way to overcome a condition. Sometimes this is true, but I will look at all my options especially where my child is concerned. If I can help the body heal by using more natural methods, even if it is more work, I choose this option. Often, we can use allopathic and naturopathic medicine simultaneously. Be responsible to do your homework to make the best decision for you and your child. Being your child's advocate means that you make smart choices by asking questions, thinking, considering and overcoming the fear of "looking dumb" or asking the "wrong" question. You seek and you ask questions until the best choice can be made. All choices have challenges that come with them. Some challenges are more difficult than others. Life in general is a series of challenges. Good parenting often presents some of our greatest challenges.

Psychiatric Medications Taken By Children

I have been increasingly concerned about the rise and overabundant usage of medication taken by children, especially psychiatric drugs. Over the last eight years, I have spoken to numerous parents who have chosen to medicate their children for various behavior conditions. By the time they end up looking for other options to help their children, their children have been exposed to the serious side effects of the psychiatric medication. Many of the parents that I have spoken with feel that their children have not done well on the medication and most of the children are experiencing other symptoms brought on by the medication. It can be appropriate to use medication if urgent care is needed for a psychiatric condition. However, don't just stop there hoping that the medication will solve the problem. There is no complete relief in a pill. I feel that in this area of health that we could be doing so much more to integrate allopathic and naturopathic medicine.

I have great respect for the research and experience of Dr. Peter Breggin M.D., who held a private practice in psychiatry for almost thirty-five years. He has not been afraid to speak up about the conspiracy of the drug companies and also organized psychiatry which have both sought larger markets for pharmaceutical products, especially for children. He has stated on his website, that the first great assault against our children was manifested in the form of diagnosing children with ADHD and then using stimulant drugs to medicate them. Now we have millions of children who are defined a mentally dysfunctional in some way, but nobody is pointing the finger at the brain-damaging psychoactive medication given to these children. These medications are so powerful that Dr. Breggin gives a strong warning on his website.

WARNING!! Most psychiatric drugs can cause withdrawal reactions, sometimes including life-threatening emotional and physical withdrawal problems. In short, it is not only dangerous to start taking psychiatric drugs, it can also be dangerous to stop them. Withdrawal from psychiatric drugs should be done carefully under experienced clinical supervision.

<u>Never</u> stop taking psychiatric medication cold turkey. These are powerful drugs and should be weaned off of carefully under professional supervision. There are many qualified and compassionate clinical professionals that will help you do this in a safe way. You have look, ask and be diligent in finding health care professionals that will help you meet you and your child's health goals. You have choices.

I don't want this book to be a medication bashing book. I do want to bring to your attention that our children are being used as pawns and as guinea pigs in a battle for power and money. If you want more information about the effects and uses of psychiatric medication concerning children, there are many resources available.

The following books by Dr. Breggin contain more detailed discussions of the use of psychiatric drugs for children:

Brain-Disabling Treatments in Psychiatry (2008)
Medication Madness (2008)
The Ritalin Fact Book (2002)
Talking Back to Ritalin (2001)
Reclaiming Our Children (2000)
The War Against Children of Color (1994)
Toxic Psychiatry (1994)

Available at: www.breggin.com

I also found the information in *A Brain Gone Wrong*, By Dr. W. Dean Belnap, very insightful and helpful.

One of my favorite books is *Healing Anxiety and Depression*, By Daniel G. Amen M.D. I have a great respect for the work that the Amen Clinic provides. They truly have found a way to integrate allopathic and naturopathic medicine. This clinic also looks at the whole person to achieve the right diagnosis and protocol for treatment. I am impressed with the SPECT imaging that is done to help analyze which parts of the brain are not functioning properly. These doctors really do care if they are prescribing the right medication, herbs, and diet for treatment of the affected part of the brain.

I believe many of you and your children may be taking medication for a disorder that has not been properly diagnosed. Your child could be taking medication which is treating parts of the brain or body that do not need treatment while neglecting parts that do. I respect doctors that look beyond the surface symptoms so that the patient has the opportunity to get well. Good doctors are not just blindly writing prescriptions. Good doctors care about your child's environment, what foods they are eating, what supplements they take, if they exercise and if they do need medication, they make sure that they are prescribing the right one. Remember, they don't call it practicing medicine for no reason. Nobody is using my kid as a guinea pig!

The Food Pyramid

Instead of medicating our children, let's do some preventive work. The most important component to building a healthy foundation for our children is to provide a healthy diet. A healthy diet looks like this:

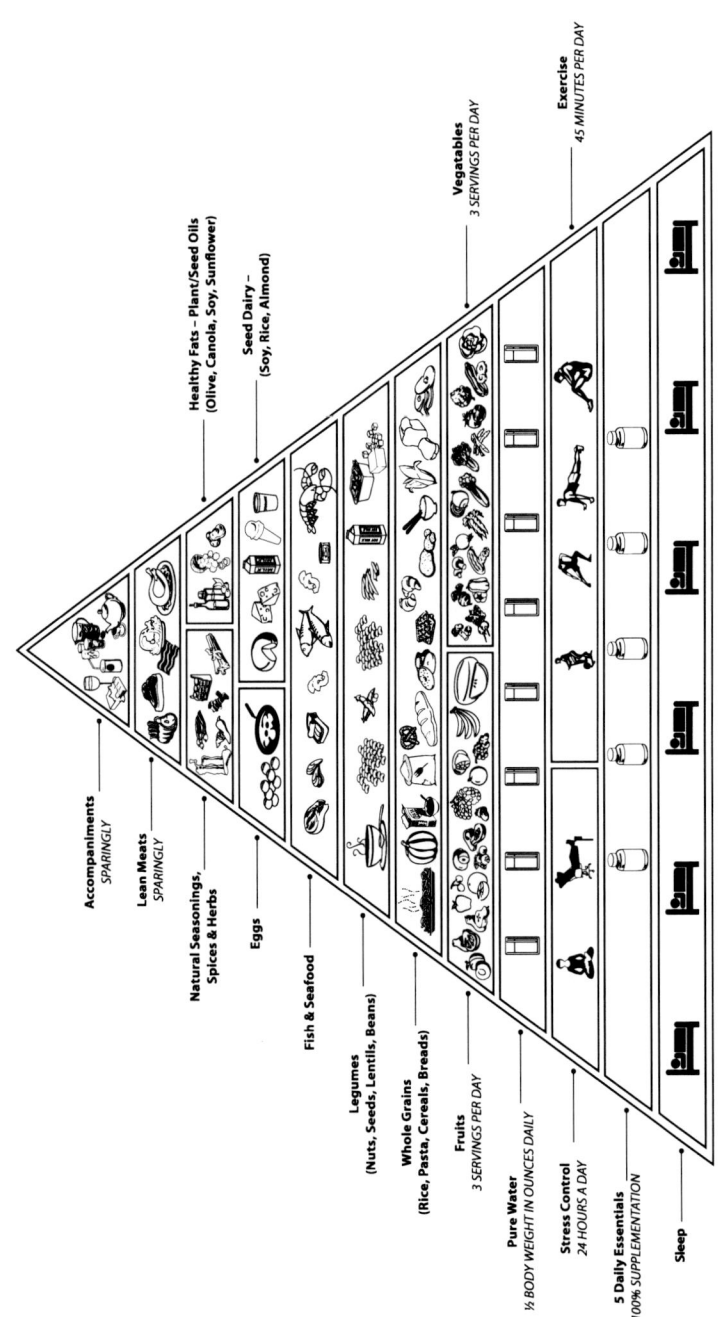

- **Accompaniments** — SPARINGLY
- **Lean Meats** — SPARINGLY
- **Natural Seasonings, Spices & Herbs**
- **Eggs**
- **Fish & Seafood**
- **Legumes** (Nuts, Seeds, Lentils, Beans)
- **Whole Grains** (Rice, Pasta, Cereals, Breads)
- **Fruits** — 3 SERVINGS PER DAY
- **Healthy Fats – Plant/Seed Oils** (Olive, Canola, Soy, Sunflower)
- **Seed Dairy** — (Soy, Rice, Almond)
- **Vegetables** — 3 SERVINGS PER DAY
- **Pure Water** — ½ BODY WEIGHT IN OUNCES DAILY
- **Exercise** — 45 MINUTES PER DAY
- **Stress Control** — 24 HOURS A DAY
- **5 Daily Essentials** — 100% SUPPLEMENTATION
- **Sleep**

I Am My Child's Advocate

Supplements help to support the body by an essential foundation for health. It is nearly impossible to get 100% nutrition from food, even the very best diets. The five daily essentials that I recommend for optimal health are:

Daily Multivitamin & Mineral: It is important to find a full-spectrum multivitamin and mineral supplement to provide support of immune system function, metabolism, digestion, nerve function and proper growth. These nutrients are also necessary for muscle and nerve function and detoxification of the liver.

Antioxidant: Keeping our families healthy is always the best choice instead of fighting off illness after we have become ill. Antioxidants are key to helping keep our immune systems healthy and strong. I recommend using an antioxidant that contains Astaxanthin, which is a super anti-oxidant many times more effective than Beta Carotene, and helps protect the body from damage by free radicals and environmental influences. I have used Astaxanthin with clients and my own family for many years with great success in warding off illness and also shortening the duration of illness or infection once one has taken hold in body.

Evening Primrose Oil: This source of Omega 6 Fatty Acids helps to lower weight without dieting, lower blood cholesterol, lower blood pressure, improve eczema, improved rheumatoid arthritis, relieved premenstrual pain, improved acne when taken with zinc, visible improvement of eczema or psoriasis, improved behavior of hyperactive children, and improved fingernail and hair growth. I have had frequent comments from clients that they notice a difference in themselves and their children when they stop taken the Evening Primrose Oil. I personally feel the same way when I haven't taken Evening Primrose Oil. I don't feel as balanced or as well when I don't take it daily. I notice a big difference in all three of my children when they take this supplement.

Flax Seed Oil: This source of Omega 3 Fatty Acids helps to increase metabolic rate, reduces the effects of harmful fatty acids, increases energy, increase stamina and muscle fatigue recovery, reduces inflammation, decrease in water retention, improves PMS and arthritis symptoms, and assists in oxygen transfer from the lungs to the blood to the tissues.

Calcium: Make sure your Calcium is packaged for solubility, preferably in a liquid or liquid gel form. Calcium provides strength to bones and teeth, works with magnesium for cardiovascular health, helps prevent Osteoporosis, acts as a natural sleep aid, helps with jumpy legs syndrome and helps to eliminate muscle cramps, including menstrual cramps. It is difficult to get the necessary milligrams of bio-available Calcium each day in a regular diet. Remember, we are not cows and cannot get the proper form of Calcium from dairy. Many individuals, especially children, are allergic to dairy and will have negative health effects from consuming dairy, some very severe. I have heard many stories from parents, many of children with ADHD and Autism that reported improved health and behavior directly after cutting out diary.

I believe that this is the minimum that our families should be supplementing every day. I also give my family extra Vitamin D for protection against cancer and Probiotics to keep friendly bacteria in the body, improve digestion and fight off Candida. My son takes Tranquility herbs every morning before school to help calm his nervous system naturally. I also give him the Tranquility herbs other times during the day if he seems hyper or unbalanced. They also work great when taken with Liquid Calcium 30 minutes before bedtime if you or your child has trouble with sleep.

Cost, Inconvenience, and Rewards

Cost and consuming so many supplements are worries for many parents. I understand these concerns. I also understand that preventative care is much cheaper and easier than having sick kids. I am self employed and have to cover the cost of health insurance 100% out of my own pocket. This, in itself, is a huge incentive to keep my family well. I haven't taken my children to the doctor for an illness in many years, so many years that the nurse at the pediatrician's office tried to verbally reprehend me for not coming in for "well checkups." I told her quite firmly that my children were well and I wasn't brining them into an office full of sick kids so that the doctor could tell me what I already knew, that my kids were well. How dumb is that?

I do not want to disillusion you that my kids are jumping up and down and begging to take their supplements. After all these years, they complain almost every day about taking them. I still have to stand and watch the vitamins be consumed so that they don't end up in pant pockets, hidden on dining room chairs, even inside of my son's socks that he is wearing! Just today, I found supplements hidden in a cupboard in the front hall! However, the benefits far outweigh being sick or having a child with an unbalanced system. It is worth every penny and all the nagging to take the supplements. I recently was able to cut my medical insurance costs down to a major medical policy which is only $181.00 a month for my entire family. It used to be almost $500.00 a month. Yes, we have a higher deductable, but hardly ever utilize the medical benefits, so we don't have to pay much out of pocket. Most doctors are happy to get a cash full payment right away and provide a nice discount. We were able to do this because of our health history and confidence in the preventive care measures we take on a daily basis. I can use the extra money we save on insurance premiums to buy the supplements that I need. In the long run it is so much less expensive to just stay well.

chapter eight:
Environmental Healing and Challenges

Your home can be a place of hell or healing. The choice is ultimately in your hands.

YES NO

☐ ☐ Do you generally yell or raise your voice loudly in order to be heard or obeyed?

☐ ☐ Are you often resorting to threats or bribes for your children to complete standard every day chores, assignments or responsibilities?

☐ ☐ Do your refrigerator and/or pantry resemble a 7-11 in its food offerings?

☐ ☐ Are you unorganized and keep a lot of "clutter" around your home?

☐ ☐ Are you late most of the time getting your kids places and picking them up?

☐ ☐ Do you and/or your kids frequently stay up late, sleep in late, or feel unrested and hurried in the mornings?

☐ ☐ Do you make excuses for your child's bad behavior in public because he or she has "behavioral challenges"?

☐ ☐ Are you more comfortable giving in to inappropriate behavior, especially in public, in order to stop a tantrum or to avoid feeling embarrassed?

☐ ☐ You do not closely monitor your child's classroom environment on a regular basis? (at least every 3 months)

☐ ☐ Do you allow your children to watch violence on T.V. or in movies?

☐ ☐ Does your child play violent video games regularly?

☐ ☐ Do you consume fast food more then one time per week? Is fast food a primary food source or a real "treat" at your house?

☐ ☐ Do your children suffer from frequent allergies, colds or flu?

☐ ☐ Does your child go more than one day without having a bowel movement?

☐ ☐ Do you use prescription medication in order to control your child's behavior?

☐ ☐ Do you engage in behaviors that you have told your child not to? Do you lead by example or only by word?

☐ ☐ Is your child living with unrealistic expectations that you or their teachers have demanded? Are you living your long lost dreams through your child?

☐ ☐ Is your child living with no expectations?

- ❏ ❏ Does family meal time consist of everyone eating different foods and different times?
- ❏ ❏ You don't provide supplements for your kids.
- ❏ ❏ You provide supplements in the form of chewable vitamins that have sugar, food coloring or dye, artificial flavoring or sweeteners.
- ❏ ❏ Your children's vitamins are in press tabs form.
- ❏ ❏ You have trouble finding babysitters because your child or children have gained a reputation as "hellions."
- ❏ ❏ Your child destroys property, including your home *(toys, walls, doors, electronics, etc.)*.
- ❏ ❏ Are you overprotective of your child? *(Do you allow your child to have new experiences and growth opportunities without you hovering in the background?)*
- ❏ ❏ Do you primarily teach your child by instilling fear instead of caution?
- ❏ ❏ I can't remember the last time my child exercised outside of P.E. class for 30 minutes or more 5 days a week.
- ❏ ❏ It has been more than a week the last time I read a book, played a game or listened to music with my child.
- ❏ ❏ I don't remember the last meaningful compliment I gave my child.
- ❏ ❏ My child acts like he or she is the parent.

Less than 5 answers marked: Your child's environment is probably mostly helpful and healing. Pick one of each of these items to improve upon every 30 days.

5 to 10 answers marked: Your child's environment is toxic to your entire family and you should implement immediate action and lifestyle changes. Pick at least 2 of these items each month that you are going to correct starting today! Be consistent!

10 to 20 answers marked: Your child's environment is not only toxic, but dangerous to your child's mind, body and spiritual development. Your child could suffer long term repercussions from the hot bed of toxic habits and behavior in your home and school surroundings. You may need to seek outside counseling to achieve your goals.

20 to 30 answers marked: Your child's environment is reminiscent of hell and most likely has virtually no healing qualities and invites bad behavior and toxic habits and life style choices. Your family has a lot of work to do in order to bring about a healthy environment in which your child can heal and thrive. You should take the 3 most urgent items and start working on them now! At least 3 new items per month should be implemented into your home. If your home is in a crisis situation you may need to implement more steps per month in order for your child to not spontaneously combust! You may need outside support and counseling to achieve your goals.

If your home is more like hell, then put out the flames. It is tough, hard, hot, dirty work, and as your child's advocate you are responsible for creating a place of healing not more heat!

Fake it till you feel it is a great place to start. Feelings will generally follow actions when practiced consistently. I am still surprised by how many people want to implement changes in the home life and in the lives of the children, but they are unwilling to do anything that doesn't come naturally. Growth opportunities are never comfortable, and don't always naturally feel good when we first encounter the challenge, otherwise, they wouldn't be growth opportunities.

One of the quickest ways our families get into trouble is by avoiding growth opportunities. Speaking plainly, this means, fake it until the actions and behaviors come more naturally. For example: Very few of my clients, especially children, jump up and down yelling give me more, supplements, soy milk, and Stevia, when they start the Candida program. However, by the end of the program they have found that some of the things they didn't care for in the beginning of the program, they have learned to enjoy. It is interesting that when good health returns, people are willing to reexamine their feelings about food and lifestyle in general. When the mask of cravings and addiction is lifted, we, children included, view food differently and more reasonably. We find that we really are not faking our feeling and behaviors anymore.

The School Rule

It's a shame that society is setting an example for our children that states that if you are uncomfortable in a new situation or more importantly, you don't like what you are doing, you don't need to stretch yourself to examine why, just do what you want to do! Eat all you want to eat. Spend all the money you want to spend and then "borrow" some more. Work as little as possible and only serve those people that society deems really "needy." Watch T.V. and play video games as much as you want to because the mindless violence probably won't have an impact on you anyway. Our children are in classrooms that are overcrowded and teaching is directed towards students at the lowest level, but we are not going to leave any child behind? What a joke. They aren't leaving anyone behind. No, it is much worse than that. "They" are downright steamrolling some of the kids, which is worse than being left behind. They are getting crushed and trampled by the very system that was put into place to help them.

We had this experience in our family. We moved to a new home and neighborhood when my youngest two children were in third and fifth grade. The public school in our neighborhood boundaries had just hired a new principal. The feedback from parents seemed positive and I was encouraged that my children would receive a decent education at this public school. My children started off in private school and due to the long drive and cost of tuition we integrated them into public school a couple of years prior to this move. All of my children are bright and they also have very different learning styles, strengths, challenges and needs.

Within the first couple of weeks at our new school, I could see that my son was struggling to complete most of his schoolwork. The teacher told me he was acting out and misbehaving. I went to great lengths to set up reward charts for good behavior and addressed the bad behavior with appropriate consequences. I did not see any improvement. I decided something was wrong, because even though my child liked attention and wanted to be in the center of everything, his behavior was out of character. I started parking my car in the parking lot by the playground and I secretly watched my children to see how they were interacting with others. I was broken hearted to see that they were not engaging in play with the other kids, again not true to character for either my children. I came to learn that the kids at this school were not particularly welcoming or accepting of new kids or some of the other students in general.

My kids and I decided to try and make new friends the creative way. I bought big bouncing balls and bags of treats for each child to start a game at recess and to give away treats to the winners. This was only mildly successful. I then stood outside my son's classroom during the day at different times and 30 minutes before school let out to see if I could overhear anything happening in his room. I did not even let his teacher know I was there. I got a lot of information! On one occasion, I heard his teacher saying to a boy in his class, "It just breaks my heart that you stomped on (Johnny's) head." I'm thinking "WHAT?!!!" What kind of kids are in this class and who has control over them? She did a lot of yelling too. After four weeks of working with the principal, the teacher, and my son, we were no further ahead. My son was miserable and my daughter was bored because she was being taught things from one to two years previous and the teacher could not or would not give her challenging work assignments.

The school wanted to test my son for learning disabilities so that they could send him to Resource, a class for children with learning difficulties. This was laughable because I had been spying on his chaotic daily experience at school, so I told them to go ahead. I knew that my son was brilliant and would test at grade level and beyond. I found out that in this third grade class, there were twenty boys and seven girls. There's a recipe for disaster right there! Seven of the kids in the class were already going to Resource and two were autistic and needed special help. There was one teacher. I don't think I can paint a clearer picture of mayhem.

In a nut shell, my son was in a toxic environment with daily chaos on all sides. The effect the room had on him was just as if he were the Tin Man in a lightening storm every day. He could not function with the toxic levels of energy in this classroom. I fully believe to this day, that some of those kids going to Resource probably did not need to even be there. They needed somebody to advocate a better learning environment for them.

I had made up my mind on a Friday that my children would not go back to this school no matter what. I was not in a position to home school and the private schools were full and also expensive, but I was willing to pay to get my kids in a better situation. When we make a true effort to help ourselves and our families and try and fail multiple times, a way is eventually provided. My way came in the form of a new neighbor who had home-schooled her children and who now had one child in a charter school. A new charter school that I didn't know existed in my city. Yes, I was able to get both of my children in that charter school on the following Monday morning in the last two open spots, one in third grade and one in fifth grade, and it happened to be the last day of open enrollment. God loves me.

I did not tell the public school we were not coming back. I just let me kids miss those first two days of the week because I was supposed to get the results back for my son's testing on that Tuesday. On Tuesday, I went to the scheduled meeting with the district specialist, principal and third grade teacher. I received the results that I expected. My son tested at or above grade level on all of his subjects with above average test scores. What a joke. I respectfully, but very firmly, explained that my children were not coming back to the school because none of our needs were being met. I turned to the third grade teacher and told her that I felt sorry for her because her classroom was so toxic that virtually no child could have a good learning experience. I told them that they were steamrolling my kid and that the environment that they allowed to exist was creating havoc in his life. I playfully punched the principal in the arm and told him he better get on the ball because his classrooms were not conducive to learning.

I later learned that this particular third grade teacher had resigned a couple of months later. I don't know that my "little speech" had any role in this decision, but I was told she was no longer there. Maybe she realized she was fighting a battle without any reinforcement, either from her principal, or from parents who were not advocating for their children's wellbeing.

My children starting thriving the first week at the new charter school, which had two teachers per classroom from kindergarten through sixth grade. Each child left their homeroom for Reading, Spelling and Math to go to classes with kids of all ages who were on their same ability level during those subjects. They were encouraged, empowered and disciplined when needed. Parents must provide a minimum of 40 hours per school year for two parent families and 20 hours for single parent families. These parents and teachers were going to be involved. Hooray!

We parents must do whatever is necessary to advocate for the right learning environment. No matter what! I know too many parents, who feel that during those school hours, that whatever happens at school is the school's problem. Last time I checked, schools weren't birthing children and women and men were responsible for bringing life into the world.

If your child is not doing well at school, look deeper than just the academic reasons. Is your child's classroom or school situation toxic? If it is, GET THEM OUT OF THERE! You may be a little inconvenienced at first, but it will fall into place and a natural rhythm of change will come about. Most importantly, your child will thrive and survive. All children weather every day challenges growing up, but being in a toxic school environment at least six hours a day crushes the emotional and spiritual health of your child, which often turns into, or magnifies physical problems.

The Ex-Challenge

I was married a little more than a week before my 22nd birthday. I was optimistic, almost to a fault, about my ability to adjust to being a step-parent to a six year old little girl, and having a stress free relationship with her biological mother. Optimism is a wonderful thing, but it does not prepare you for many of the challenges that lay ahead of you, it only helps you to view the challenges from a more positive perspective.

I suspected from the beginning I was not going to be liked very much by my husband's ex-wife for several reasons. First, I was seven years younger than my husband, which made me "the younger woman." Second, her daughter really liked me and we had a lot of fun together, which made me seem a little threatening. I think the most annoying to her was that I was happy, upbeat and cheerful toward her at all times, which I am sure was really irritating! In hindsight, I was probably super annoying!

I decided from the beginning, after watching many people make many mistakes, that I was going to use the "kill 'em with kindness" approach. Although, at times, I thought it might kill me instead. It is often difficult to be nice when you want to be right, first, or just plain better. These are forms of insecurity that can damage your relationship with your children, stepchildren, spouse, or ex-spouse. I recognized that I was only in charge of myself, not his ex-wife, and not my husband. I did not want to become ugly on the inside by harboring resentment, hatred, or jealousy. I came up with a plan. The plan works, not because I had intended to change anybody other than myself. If you set out to change others, this does not work. If you set out to improve yourself, then others often improve with you in the process. Here's the plan:

Every time I was irritated with a situation involving my husband's ex-wife, I did something for her. I baked her bread or cookies. I wrote her a note or sent her a card telling her what a good mother she was. I brought samples home from the cosmetic counter where I worked at the time to give to her. I offered to bake birthday cakes, shared recipes, and gave her mother, who is suffering from Parkinson's disease, supplements. I did anything that would help me serve her and understand her better. It is difficult to harbor bad feelings towards those whom we serve. Service is healing.

Pretty soon I stopped worrying so much about where I was fitting into this picture of parenthood, and I could see the benefits of placing this child before all other desires to be noticed, be right, or to be recognized. Guess what? The ex-wife called me about three months after my wedding and told me that she did not want to like me, but that she couldn't help herself because I was too nice! Sixteen years later, I believe she still likes me and I like her. She turned to me over the years, when we needed to make decisions about our daughter. She called on me when she needed support or backing in a parental stance she had taken. Things were not always smooth, but they were respectful and communication was open. You can't ask for more than that. I received a lovely condolence card from her when my brother passed away a couple of years ago. The best part of the whole experience was that I was internally peaceful and could look for the good in her, myself, and my husband.

The whole point of this section is that environment matters. We, as parents, have to advocate for change in our children's environment if it is toxic in any way. Sometimes we are the ones making the environment toxic. Divorce and mixed families seem to be all too common today. If you are in a mixed family situation, then make sure you examine yourself on a regular basis. Remember, fake it till you feel it? This applies here. You are in control of only one person, you. We need to do everything we can to keep our families in tact, even if it means that we are not happy or getting everything we think we want or desire. Other than abuse of any kind, we need to advocate in keeping our families together. If your spouse is not doing anything immoral, illegal, or abusive, then you need to find a way to heal your home environment for your children's sake. Selfishness on our part creates environmental toxicity in our homes. If you are a toxic parent then STOP today! Only you can change and improve yourself and your children's future environment, and the good news is that it's free. It's free to change yourself so that your have freedom to be an advocate for your children.

chapter nine:
Powerful Parenting

The Power of Always

I have been amused by the murmurings of my children over the years. If I have done anything more than one time, my children say that I *always* do that one thing. This is true if it is good or bad. My husband raises his voice in frustration every once in a while when home rules have been broken or the kids have are not behaving as they know they should behave. My children will tell you that he *always* yells at them. They will also tell you that their dad *always* plays chess with them, even though he only does that sometimes too. I *always* make homemade rolls for Sunday dinner, I *always* try to "fix" my kids problems instead of just listening, and I also *always* travel for my job, even though the latter rarely happens anymore. You get the point. So use the power of always to your advantage. If you practice spending more time with your children, really listening to them, sticking up for them when they are the underdog, or going to bat for them in a toxic school environment, they will remember that you *always* did these things. If you often seem too busy for your children, leave them to fend for themselves in toxic settings, feed them fast food and junk food frequently, or are late picking them up from school or lessons, then you will be remembered as *always* doing these things.

I am trying to shape what I will be remembered always doing, knowing I have a hand in these memories that my children are making. I want to be remembered always:

- Advocating for my children's educational environment.
- Reading to my children and loving books.
- Being tough when it comes to doing your best work.
- Loving God and having gratitude for all that I have been given.
- Teaching my kids good manners.
- Inspiring confidence in my children's abilities and talents.
- Listening.
- Serving others.

- Being available.
- Teaching my children to be responsible for their own health.
- Being a good example regarding financial stability and security.
- Having a sense of humor.

I can remember reciting memories of childhood vacations and everyday living circumstances in front of my parents. My parents would frequently comment that they didn't remember certain situations the way that I did. My mother brought up the point that she did not always sing cheerfully every morning while playing classical music to get us up and ready for school while turning on the lights! However, I remembered her always doing this even though she probably only did it a few times. I also remember her always playing the rhyming game with me on long trips. We also always went to church every Sunday. My always memories of growing up are almost all good, funny, and loving. I want my children's memories to be the same way and I have to be aware that what I choose to do and not do will be always remembered just that way. The power of never works the same way as the power of always so be care not to create an environment of "you (we) never" did this or that when raising your kids.

The Power of Prayer

I believe that if we could see the prayers to God ascending to the heavens, we would see that the most powerful, the brightest, the most intense prayers came from mothers and fathers who were praying on behalf of their children. These prayers are packed with love, pain, desperation, gratitude, joy, and sorrow. Sometimes we feel that mighty intervention is the only way that we can save or help our children and we turn pleading to God to step in and take over. What we don't realize is that he's already in charge, and we are just not happy with the natural consequences or the challenges that have come our way, not necessarily because of choices that we have made or even choices our children have made. Sometimes it is just the challenge itself that God wants us to grow from. I have pondered this thought often as I have been faced with hurdles in raising my kids. I don't know that I am always victorious in my outcome, but I sure do straighten my backbone and square my shoulders in an effort to carry the load that may be placed on me. I am also convinced that I will win the challenge and overcome whatever may be placed in our way. You may have to dig deep, but you too, can know that there is a plan and God is in charge of it. You are not parenting alone, you have Him. Every child deserves parents who will pray on their behalf. You just can't have too much help in raising your kids, especially that kind of help.

Unique Circumstances and Trials

It is so easy to compare our trials and suffering to someone else's. Although, our trials and suffering may not be unique, how we choose to handle them may be. We can take comfort knowing that the challenges of parenthood which await us have been experienced before, usually by many. We must also recognize that we all experience pain, loss, and challenges in our own way. I strongly caution using phrasing that says, "I know exactly how you feel," or "I know just what you are going through." These statements can appear to the person struggling, that you are focusing attention on yourself and/or diminishing the importance of what is happening to the parents or child having the difficulty.

Many times we have to experience our parenting challenges in stages, and when individuals are in certain stages of coping they don't want to hear that what is happening to them is anything but devastating. They are certain that they feel worse than anybody has ever felt in their situation. They may even move through the stages of: The Sufferer, The Arguer, and finally, hopefully, The Doer. If you catch people in the first two stages, comfort should be your main goal. When you catch somebody in the Doer stage they seem more willing to listen to suggestions about how to forge ahead while facing adversities. This goes back to being teachable, and some people never get to this point, sad, but true. The whole point is that we don't need to compare in order to be compassionate.

Advocating by Using Our Talents

We all have different and special talents, which I believe were given to us to uplift others and create balance. When we are truly seeking solutions to our parenting challenges, we can utilize our talents. Yes, we all have at least one, to creatively help solve problems. Think about the story I told at the beginning of the book about the tent. You may have different parenting talents than I do, but that is why you were given the children that you have, because YOU are the perfect person, who has been given the perfect abilities to help your child.

Your parental talent(s) may be patience, tolerance, foresight, creativity, endurance, spiritual insight, intelligence, strength, playfulness, or consistency. These are just a few parental talents that we can be blessed with. Most of us have more than one. I believe we have been given our special parental talents in order to help our specific children. Here is a story that my mother sent me that was printed in Meridian Magazine, and I just love that illustrates this point. You might be shocked, but read the whole story!

"Dear Larry,

I am the mother of six children—four girls and two boys—all born during a nine year span. Because they were close in age, one child's behavior had an affect all the rest. We were a close family. We had a boat, water-skied, snow-skied, hiked, and played together. We also all worked together; cleaned house and did the yard work, with everyone assigned part of the task. We went to church every Sunday, and were a close-knit family, in a healthy, happy way. My husband was a good man; a good husband and father. However, his job required that he go out of town frequently, and I was often dealing with our children on my own.

The oldest boy, Scott (name changed), had been a difficult child, from the time he was a baby. It was exhausting to be his mother. He was my 4th child, so it wasn't that I was inexperienced, but I went to bed exhausted, night after night, from dealing with him. He drained more of my energy than the other five children. He seemed to delight in tormenting his younger brother and sisters. When a particular older sister walked into a room where he was, the instant tension was palpable, and all of us felt it. We couldn't even hold Family Night for more than a few minutes without his disrupting everything. It was daily chaos.

One night, in despair, I wondered if we should send him to a foster home. It was a shock to me that I had even thought of something like that. But Scott's behavior just wasn't fair to the other five children; it wasn't right that they should suffer unrelenting torment. That night I prayed earnestly to know if sending him to a foster home was the right answer. I was at my wit's end, and I was desperate to find a rational answer. I asked the Lord why Scott had come to our family.

Then the answer quietly came into my heart and mind: The Spirit whispered that I was the only one who would love him no matter what he did, and that he needed to have every opportunity to succeed in this life. I was to give him that. It was a profound answer that soothed my troubled heart, and encouraged me to look for other ways to work with my son. (This woman utilized the power of prayer and inspired, she practiced using her parental talents.)

My husband and I went to work. We had to teach him discipline and responsibility without breaking his spirit. With a lot of prayer and hard work, we made it through his teenage years. After that, he still had years of ups and downs, and trials, mostly of his own making. He will turn 40 soon. He is now married and has a cute family. He is a wonderful husband and father. It gives me so much joy to see him amazingly happy and more contented than I had once thought he could possibly be. His wife is perfect for him, and we all love her so much. We all love Scott, too, like we always wanted to. Now when our family gets together, it is truly a joyous occasion. We have love in our home."

Once Devastated and Now Grateful Mother

chapter ten:
Parenting with a Purpose

Gratitude for Grandparents

It may just be me, but is there an epidemic of grandparents raising their grandchildren these days? I remember when I was growing up that there were a couple of kids that lived with their grandparents, but maybe just one or two. Now days, it seems as though, this is very common. Some grandparents are solely raising their grandkids, while others are "jointly" raising grandchildren in conjunction with their own children. Many of these adult children want their parents to be glorified babysitters, and they don't want to be told how to raise their children. Well I say, "Get your own house then, pay your own way, and hire a babysitter!"

If you are lucky enough to have parents that want to be involved with their grandchildren, listen, and be respectful, you might learn something. It doesn't mean you have to do everything they tell you to do, but be teachable. I certainly don't think when raising your children, that you want to make all of your own mistakes. You are going to make mistakes anyway, so you may as well learn from those who came before you. There are some things that are timeless and never change when it comes to raising kids and there are some environmental changes that need to be considered differently as our world evolves. We have spoken about some of them, TV, internet, and psychiatric drugs, to name a few.

It might be possible that you need your parent's assistance to get "back on your feet." Make sure you use the principal of gratitude when accepting their help with your children. This is part of being an advocate for your children, not loosing sight of the gift of wisdom, experience, and love that comes from good grandparents. I realize that not all grandparents are good. Some are toxic and damaged, but we are not talking about these grandparents. Toxic and/or damaged persons, related or not, should be kept away from your children at all times. If your family encounters a situation with a toxic relative, contact should be 100% monitored and kept very limited in duration.

Roadblocks

Grandparents have a different struggle than parents. Grandparents have the experience, hindsight, foresight, and wisdom to be helpful in guiding their grandchildren as they are growing up. The struggle many grandparents are experiencing is that their adult children often put up roadblocks which hinder the grandparents help.

Roadblocks that occur when adult children are living with or receiving help from their children's' grandparents:

- Ongoing power struggles between the adults.
- The adult child is a poor planner.
- Immaturity on the part adult child.
- Laziness on the adult child's part.
- Irresponsibility of the adult child.
- Adult child is just plain selfish.
- Household rules and expectations have not been established.
- Grandchildren have not been given the rules, goals, or expectations.
- The household rules have not been consistently enforced with the grandchildren.
- Goals and an exit plan for adult children and grandchildren to become independent again have not been made, especially before combining household.

I have become less resistant to suggestions from my parents as I have aged. I now actively seek their advice and use them as a sounding board as I make decisions regarding my own children. I am far from knowing it all and I appreciate the insight of parents who love my children, love me, and seek all of our best interest. Again, being teachable means that you listen, consider, research, and then make the best decision you can with the information that you have, which includes advice from loving grandparents, especially, if you have entrusted the care of your children to them.

Grandparents are not always around their grandchildren and sometimes grandchildren will listen to grandparents long after they have tuned parents out, because they hear the parents every day. Grandparents also use different methods of communication with their grandchildren, than the parents do, because the relationship is different. Through this different relationship, communication channels can be strengthened and we can get a fresh perspective from people whom we trust.

My children call my mother "Golden Grandma" because she used to drive a gold Jeep Grand Cherokee, and because she treats them like gold, a precious valuable treasure. This does not mean that she lets them get away with any shenanigans, or disrespect. My parents discipline my children if they need it and teach them manners and priceless life lessons. I want my parents to know that when they have my children that respect of their rules and obedience is expected and that they have every right to enforce those expectations.

Being an advocate for your child means giving them as many supportive, loving people in their lives as you can to provide a solid foundation. Loving grandparents are part of this foundation. If you don't have loving parents, then adopt other loving adults into your family's life. The world is full of people that would love to give service and will embrace you in your efforts to be an advocate for your child.

Normal Stuff is Good Stuff

I am as guilty as many of you are of over scheduling my family. This is just not good. As an advocate for my child, I realize that I need to leave room for "normal stuff." What is normal stuff? Normal stuff can simply be quiet, reflective time to regroup or to play with friends. Remember what playing with friends was like? A lot of children have no idea what this really means anymore because they are so busy running from one structured activity to another. My best childhood memories came from playing with friends all summer and after school and I don't ever, even in high school, remember having the enormous amount of homework that kids have today. I think the schools should forget all that extra homework, (aren't they going to school for 6 hours a day?) and start helping these kids get healthy, mind, body and spirit. Let's start encouraging and developing our kid's specific interests and talents during these formative years.

We have way too many wayward children in toxic environments. I would love to see programs that stimulate natural interests and aptitudes encouraged, instead dishing out all of this extra homework. It's just a part of the "We Are Steamrolling Your Kid" program, or better known as, "No Child Left Behind." This program will be renamed something else in a few years as it seems to keeps coming around as a facade to keep us under the illusion that something is being done to help our children in the school system. How many of you parents are the "puppet master" behinds your kids success? Are you a big part of the homework process and the master mind behind your kid's projects? Guilty, I have done it in order to relieve some of the time burden and aggravation. Being an advocate, we need to work to change what is happening in our children's classroom and schools. Nothing will change unless we speak up and advocate for something different and better.

Good Normal Stuff

- Eating dinner together as a family.
- Playing with friends, preferably outside doing something active.
- Reading a good book.
- Playing a board game with friends or siblings.
- Cooking treats in the kitchen.
- Setting up a lemonade stand in the neighborhood.
- Playing with the family pet.
- Taking a nap.
- Enjoying a hobby or interest uninterrupted.

These are just a few of the normal activities that our kids are missing out on. Normal stuff does not mean sitting mindlessly in front of the TV, computer, or playing videos games for hours. A little of those activities go a long way. Let's focus on more activities that nurture our children's positive sense of self. As my child's advocate, I am constantly reevaluating how I am doing, and sometimes, I am doing great in these areas, and sometimes, I have let things get off track and I have to regroup. It's not about being perfect, it's about awareness and making the effort to improve and never giving up the opportunity to do a better job raising your kids.

Being consistent is one of the most important tools we have as a parent. Consistency brings a sense of wellbeing and security in knowing that there are certain things our children can count on from us as parents. When we are inconsistent we lose a foothold in the foundation we are setting in place. Consistency in action and word bring strength to your relationship with your child. Being consistent isn't always fun or joyful, but it can be very rewarding down the road as we look back and see the values we sought to instill take hold and bloom, although, this may take years.

Keeping Yourself Healthy

One of the most powerful ways to advocate for your child is to get healthy and keep yourself healthy. This is a way of showing respect and advocacy for your family. It is difficult, almost impossible, to inspire your family to get well, mind, body, and spirit if you are sick and unhealthy yourself. If are unwilling and whinny about making the changes yourself, that you want your family to make, then you will not have success in helping them to get well. Lead the way with your example and enthusiasm.

When you are healthy, you will be a better EVERYTHING, including a better:

- Parent
- Employee
- Friend
- Neighbor
- Spouse
- Sibling
- Boss

We are able to focus our energies on helping others, accomplishing our goals and daily tasks when we are well and not focusing on our own ailments and suffering. We are functioning at a lower level in our lives when we are constantly focused on ourselves. In order to progress and function at a higher level, we need to be well so that we can shift the focus off of ourselves and onto others. When we have gratitude and serve we are striving to live at a higher level. In order to advocate for our children, we need to be living at this higher level.

Let's simplify what this means. Would you take weight loss advice from an obese person? Would you take wellness advice from a sick individual? Would you take advice on optimism and enthusiasm from a person who yells a lot, complains frequently, and is depressed? Enough said. My mother taught me that "If you act enthusiastic, you'll be enthusiastic." She taught me this by chanting this saying while jumping around the coffee table in our living room. However, the greatest example she taught me was by being enthusiastic throughout her life. Enthusiasm is contagious! Lead with love, enthusiasm, consistency, and your good example. Advocate for your child by advocating for yourself and then teaching them to do the same thing

Summary

- Use your parental instinct. If you think something is not quite right with your child or your child's diagnosis, you are probably right.
- Screen your child for Candida. By eating the right foods you will be making the most important step in helping your child overcome chronic health conditions and teaching life long life style choices.
- Provide good quality supplements every day for your child so that 100% nutrition is achieved and you are taking good preventative measures to avoid detrimental health conditions.
- Cut out or greatly reduce the influence of constant electronic stimulation.
- Plan for you and your spouse to get healthy before you conceive.
- Don't induce labor unless medically necessary. Be responsible. Be patient.
- Remove your child immediately from any toxic environments. There is always another choice... find it.

- Make your home a place of healing, mind, body and spirit.
- Cherish good grandparent help and find other solid adult role models to help teach your children.
- Get the family on a regular sleep schedule.
- Be on time and keep a regular schedule as much as possible.
- Write goals with your child.
- Pray for and with your child.
- Provide service opportunities for you and your child to participate in.
- Practice the principals of gratitude every day with your child.
- Keep yourself healthy and lead by example, word and deed.
- Make time for "normal stuff" that allows your child to have down time.
- Make use of your parental talents, you have more than one, so let them shine!
- Remember that the power of always is part of childhood, so always make good memories!
- Don't compare your child's struggles to others. Your family's struggles are your own and were given to you so that you could use your unique abilities to overcome them.

Let us raise up generations of healthy and responsible children. We can not afford to be passive in the teaching and guiding of our kids. If we are not actively seeking to make a difference our children's lives each day, society will raise and influence our children in ways that will have detrimental impact on everyone. You are your child's advocate, now act like it!

References

Beneficial International, The M'lis Company, 1780 W. 500 S., Salt Lake City, Utah 84104

Lack of Sleep in Late Pregnancy May Influence Length of Labor, Type of Delivery. University of California, San Francisco. Available at http://pub.ucsf.edu/today/news. Accessed December 3, 2008.

Sleep During Pregnancy. KidsHealth for Parents website. Available at: www.kidshealth.org. Accessed December 4, 2008.

Newsweek Magazine, July 31, 2000, Referenced in *The Brave New World of Evidence Maternity Care for 21 Century.* Accessed on December 4, 2008.

Care in Normal Birth: A Practical Guide—W.H.O's "Safe Motherhood" series and Mothering Magazine, Spring Issue, 2001, Referenced in *The Brave New World of Evidence Maternity Care for 21 Century.* Accessed on December 4, 2008

The Brave New World of Evidence-based Maternity Care for 21st Century, Chapter 10 ~ Autism and Pitocin Induction. Available at www.collegeofwidwives.org. Accessed on December 4, 2008.

"*The Risk to Children Using Electronic Games*", Valdemar W. Setzer, Professor of Computer Science, Institute of Mathematics and Statistics, University of São Paulo, Brazil, George E. Duckett, (at that time) Ph.D. Candidate, Faculty of Education, Deakin University, Australia. (This paper was presented as a poster paper at the Asia Pacific Information Technology in Training and Education Conference and Exhibition, 28 June – 2 July 1994, Brisbane, Australia.) Available at www.ime.usp.br/~vwsetzer/video-g-risks.html. Accessed on December 15, 2008.

"*Cytogenetic effects in children treated with methylphenidate*". El-Zein R.A., et al. (2005). Cancer Lett. 2005 Available at http://en.wikipedia.org/wiki/December_18. December 18;230(2):284-91

Ritalin and Cocaine http://learn.genetics.utah.edu/content/addiction/issues/ritalin.html

Pretreatment with methylphenidate sensitizes rats to the reinforcing effects of cocaine http://www.udel.edu/chemo/teaching/CHEM465/SitesF02/Prop26b/Rit%20Page4.html

Psychiatric Drugs and Your Children, Dr. Peter Breggin M.D. Available at www.breggin.com. Accessed on January 13, 2009.

Once Devastated and Now Grateful Mother, Meridian Magazine, by Larry Barkdull. Available at www.meridianmagazine.com. Accessed on March 31, 2009.

Airola, Paavo, Ph.D. *How to Get Well,* Sherwood: Health Plus, 1995.

Balch, Phyllis A., CNC, and James F. Balch, M.D. *Prescription for Nutritional Healing*. 3rd ed. P 717-18. New York: Avery, 2000.

Immune System and Juicing References

Calbom, Cherie, MS, CN, and Maureen Keane, MS, CN. *Juicing For Life*. Garden City Park: Avery Publishing Group Inc, 1992.

Cousens, Gabriel, M.D. *Conscious Eating*. p 233-34, 298-304, 1003. Berkeley: North Atlantic Books, 2000.

Haas, Elson M., M.D. *Staying Healthy with Nutrition*. p 986, 999. Berkeley: Celestial Arts, 1990.

Hass, Elson M., M.D. *Staying Healthy with the Seasons*. p 52, 135. Berkeley: Celestial Arts, 1981

Jensen, Bernard, D.C., Ph.D., *Dr. Jensen's Juicing Therapy: Nature's Way to Better Health and a Longer Life*. Los Angeles: Keats Publishing, 2000.

Notes

Notes

Notes